Coming Home to the Mother
A Story of Miracles
And
Teachings
Of the Blessed Virgin Mary
For
The People of Today

Janine Lariviere, MA, LMHC

Copyright © 2013 by Janine Lariviere

All rights reserved, including the scanning, uploading, and electronic sharing of any part of this book without the permission of the author or publisher. Such use will constitute unlawful piracy and theft of the author's intellectual property. If you would like to use material from the book, please contact the author at:

info@www.cominghometothemother.com.

ISBN: 978-1-892426-44-4

For all who have suffered from childhood sexual abuse and for all those who work to open their hearts to the healing presence of Our Lady

Acknowledgments

The greatest source of love and guidance for this book has come from the grace of the Blessed Virgin Mary. She chose me, a victim of ritualistic sexual abuse with a walled-off heart, to be her hands in order to use my story to "teach" of her love for all her children. As you read this book, you will be blessed with her understanding of that love just as she has blessed me. Dear Blessed Mother of all, there are no words to express the gratitude of not only saving my life, but also for bringing your loving heart into my heart.

This journey would never have been possible without the loving, patient, and prayerful help of my therapist, Dr. Donald Favreau. The first day I met him I instinctively knew (as did the alter personalities) of his patient and nurturing ways. What I did not know at the time was the journey that would unfold over the course of over two decades. Never was there a question of money or a question of his dedication to the healing ministry. I also did not know when we met that the Blessed Virgin had her hand and her loving heart on both of us. To Don, there are no words to describe my gratitude for all your years of devotion to the work that you do with such patience and love.

In those first few years, as alter personalities made themselves known in therapy, I was supported by a loving school nurse. She carried me in those times when therapy seemed unbearable as each week would bring more and more "unknowns" that each alter personality would share with Don. Cis Stientra was there in the times my world would crumble and to her I am eternally grateful.

My life would not have been manageable or bearable if I did not have the love of the two most bright and beautiful daughters a mother could ever want. In those times when I would "disappear into a walled-off shell," they were always there waiting for me when I returned. I thank the Blessed Virgin daily for them, not only for their beauty and open hearts, but also for the children they have brought into life who also honor our loving Father.

Lastly and most importantly, I wish to thank my husband Ed who has been my "rock" for forty seven years. He has been a loving and stable force in my life even when I could not see or feel it and to you, my priceless husband, I dedicate this book. May the Blessed

Virgin make a special place for you in heaven for your sincere and unwavering love.

Table of Contents

Introduction..3
A Therapist's Perspective...7
Journal Writings Prior to Mary's Visitation..11
First Meetings with the Blessed Virgin..21
Integration of alters with the help of Our Lady..................................27
Mother Explains the Role of Sin, Shaping and the Ego....................47
A Special Blessing From the Father..55
More on the Santeria..57
God's Plan for all His Children..67
The Way of the Gift..71
Mother Speaks of Hate and Hell..73
The Cleansing...79
Saying Goodbye to Sarah and Bethany..89
A Birthing into the True Meaning of Love..95
Mother Speaks of Visionaries...115
Mother Speaks of her Sick Children..117
The Pain that "Growed-up Janine" has had to Feel..........................125
Mother Speaks of the Taliban...143
The Inner Road to the Holy Spirit..147
Mother Tells of the Father's Garden...159
The Energy of Prayer and Fasting..165
"Coming Home to the Mother" Detailed...169
Mother Again Speaks of the Taliban..175
Mother Teaches of the Role of Self Love and the Ego....................179
Mother Speaks of the Evil in the Media..187
Our "Flowing Relationship" and the Flow of the Book...................191
The Way to the Father in Today's World...197

Mother Shows me her Heart..201
The Story of my Illegitimacy and the Dissociative Process..................205
The Role of "Longings"...211
The Terror of not Having Enough...215
The Way of Miracles...219
The Father's Love Despite our Choices..229
Mother Speaks of Worldly Chaos...233
The True Coming Home to the Father..237
Mother's Prayer for all Souls..243
The Misguidedness of Adam and Eve Explained..................................245
The Ways of a Loving Family..249
The Steps in Coming Home to the Mother..253
The Miracle of the Feather...277

Introduction

Introduction

It began on a quiet early spring day in 1986. I had everything in my life going so well and as I sat and looked around me I became aware of the wonderful family, the great job, and the beautiful home I have, everything that one could want in life. Yet it became increasingly difficult to be a wife, a mother, a friend and a manager of the local school food service program. I became more and more distant to the point where a close friend noticed and suggested I seek therapy. She introduced me to a wonderful therapist named Don. That was the very beginning of a long and healing journey that has gotten me to this day, this journey and this book.

After over 25 years of looking at a traumatic past and a number of alter personalities (the "alter children" were contained in the therapy hour), after going back to college with my daughters and becoming a Licensed Mental Health Counselor with a private practice, and after a dangerous surgery, I met the Blessed Virgin Mary.

This is a story of not only a painful past but also of miracles and hope that all might find wholeness in the presence of The Holy Spirit. I was fortunate enough to have the Blessed Virgin come to my aid.

The first time I met the Blessed Virgin (I knew of her through being raised as a Catholic, but she was a lost entity to me) was in a dream. My illness began in early May of 2012. I was told I needed surgery and it might possibly be ovarian cancer. A few nights before the surgery the Blessed Virgin told me in a dream she was going to be at the surgery as was the Holy Family. Her words were comforting and I knew all would be well. After that she made me more and more aware that she was a presence in my life. As you read the first sections of the book, you will get a scenic view of how she teaches me the difference between her voice and the "noise."

This book has no organization into chapters but rather sub titles based on Mother's writings. It is a story being told chronologically because that is the way the Blessed Virgin writes. In the beginning you do not see quotation marks around her words but, as you will see, she makes me aware of the need to do so because she wants the world to know that the writings are hers. Rather than use

Introduction

traditional quotation marks, I have italicized her words throughout the entire book by a bolder font in order to make it clear which of the writings are Mother's and which are mine. This makes for a better flow throughout the book.

There are some graphic details into the abuse I experienced. The Blessed Virgin has asked that I do not filter her writings because of the need to use my woundedness to teach of the Father's blessings not only upon me but also upon his people of today.

The Picture on the cover is a sketch that I did a few years ago. I began to sketch a face that turned into a likeness of what I felt looked like the Blessed Virgin. I have never had any talent with drawing but felt compelled to try and it is the only piece that I have ever done. I have tried to reproduce it and cannot to this day. The picture represents the first of the many miracles from the Blessed Virgin.

Our Lady as depicted by Janine

A Therapist's Perspective

A Therapist's Perspective

In May of 1986 a 39 year old woman came to me for therapy. She was married, had two daughters and worked in a school cafeteria. She felt her life should be good, but fears and disturbing dreams were welling up in her. As a clinical psychologist and pastoral counselor, I had no idea that this healing journey would unfold with dimensions and avenues so deeply buried, yet eventually able to surface with profound truth and healing.

In the early stages of treatment, Janine began to share deepening anxiety and fear. At times she would curl up in a fetal position and release intense screams. Eventually there was a surfacing of what the fears and pain carried. How the source of such pain came to light opened the door to what was a lifesaving "gift" of dissociation. After a period of time Dissociative Identity Disorder (formerly Multiple Personality Disorder) was the clinical diagnosis.

The fears started to center on fears of men, discomfort and insecurity in their presence. After a period of time, alters started to surface in the sessions. As each alter tested me for trust and belief, they shared their names and some aspect of what trauma Janine had experienced as a child. Each alter started to use Janine's adult body to release some of the horrific pain and anguish. During many of these incidents the adult Janine had no recall and would ask me what had "come out." Each alter, after a period of time and after sharing what part of the dissociation it carried, would in a way "die" and somehow integrate with Janine. Every alter gave a departing message that "growdup"Janine would have to feel the pain. This proved true as, after years of struggle and denial, the adult Janine did feel all the pain and eventually accepted the truth of what happened to her.

In my clinical practice I have never witnessed so much pain and terror be felt and released from one person's body, psyche and soul. After some years of therapy the adult Janine shared that Mary, the Mother of Jesus, taught her how to dissociate in order to survive the horrors of sexual and ritual abuse. From that day her therapy surfaced a dimension beyond just clinical and a spiritual component was now present.

This spiritual component included Janine using terms like

A Therapist's Perspective

"rapture" and Jesus "sanctioning" Mary to be present to Janine from the very beginning of her abuse. In one session Janine experienced what she termed a "rapture" with Abba, God the Father. In reading Theresa of Avila's description of her rapture, Janine's experience was similar.

In the fall of 2012 Janine was to have serious surgery and was filled with fear as it might be cancer. She shared that Mary came to her in a dream and assured Janine that she would be with her during the surgery. The surgery went well. Afterwards Janine shared in a session that Mary wanted to be her teacher. This was followed by Mary asking Janine to start writing and that Mary, Mother, would use Janine's hands. Since then the volume and content of Mary's message through Janine defies a simple rational explanation.

Clinically, one might assess that Mother was just a higher form of an alter, a more advanced level of integration. It's true that Janine has achieved a remarkable level of integration and continues to progress. Her level of confidence and capacity to function as a therapist herself have resulted in a full time practice.

Yet, if anyone reads the writings of Janine in "Coming Home to the Mother," one will be challenged to limit an explanation to only a natural phenomena of healing. The challenge will be frustrating until one opens up to the supernatural, transrational, mystical---whatever term might express the transcendent---presence of Mary, the Mother of God.

The writings are a humble and heroic exposure of one woman who shares her healing from sexual abuse and especially ritual sexual abuse. They also unfold the spiritual foundation of healing. For Janine it is the presence of Mother, Mary. The teachings of Mary given through Janine for the world today are a revelation and source of hope for all who have been abused. Above all, the writings reinforce the revelation of God, Abba, as a loving Father concerned and involved in every person's life journey.

As a clinical psychologist I have witnessed a healing journey that started with a woman who for all intent should have been destroyed psychologically, but is ongoing in ways that continue to defy traditional limits. As a pastoral counselor I have witnessed the power of God's presence at the foundation of healing. My faith has deepened during this journey. My faith accepts the real presence of Mary, the Mother of God, as she continues to send a message to our generations through Janine.

Anyone who reads "Coming Home to the Mother" will find hope for healing, whatever his or her spiritual relation to one's Higher Power. If one reads Janine's writings with no faith, perhaps one will be challenged to discover a belief in a personal loving God who can send Mary into the life of Janine and into anyone's life.

Donald A Favreau, D.Min. Licensed Psychologist/Provider

Journal Writings Prior to Mary's Visitation

August 1, 2012

My therapy session with Don today was extremely painful. The memory of my father giving me Paregoric before sexually abusing me brought up another memory of his giving me over to other men. Dear God, this is such a hard process. As the alter personalities give me their story, the lines between us get thinner and thinner. Soon I will have all the memories, I think, but for now as positive as the process is, (Don says it is) it is extremely painful. I can now smell and taste the Paregoric from so long ago. I don't know who the men were but I certainly see their faces.

As I think of the men, I think of auntie's house and the walkway across the street to the statue of the Blessed Virgin. I know something happened there but not sure what exactly did happen. I know that one of the alter children told Don of the "sacrifice of animals" there, but I have no memory of it. I do remember going into auntie's house and having a special place there. My place was in the corner of the alcove with the dogs and I was forced to eat out of the bowl with them as well as eat the dog food. I was also stripped naked a good portion of the time. Humiliation was her way of making sure I stayed quiet.

Dear auntie, what drove you to do these things? What drove you to continually tell me I am only fit to eat with the animals because I am an animal? Didn't you know that a child learns to see herself the way an adult makes her feel? Didn't you know that the humiliation is carried throughout her life? Why did we make trips to the Virgin? I know that you took me, "one of the twins," and my mother kept the other twin, but why? Why me? Was it because you lost a set of twins yourself and you talked my mother into taking one of us as your own? Why did you feel the need to bury my doll with your twins? Why did you feel the need to take away my humanness and relegate me to the cubby with the dogs? Do you know that I still feel like an animal today and still ask Don to explain what it feels like to be human? Where did you come from to carry this kind of hate? You took your younger brother in (my daddy) when your mother died. He was six years old. Did you teach him to hate me too? Did you teach him about how to sexually abuse me

Journal Writings Prior to Mary's Visitation

and give me over to other men, the men on the hill?

I surely remember auntie's house but the house of my parents and siblings is a blur. I do not remember having a room there until the first grade at least and yet, when as an adult I began to ask them if I was "given away," no one admitted it. But the alter children knew and eventually family friends noted as such.

Daddy, as I ponder the Paregoric, I think of all the pain of not only being sexually abused by you but also the insanity of having you give me over to other men. Yet, when we were alone, you told me you are the only man that has rights to me. Didn't you know that I would carry that all my life and never really be able to give myself wholly to Ed? You still have me in your grasp even today as Ed pays for your sins. Didn't you know, daddy, I had to wall off my heart so as to not let anyone or anything else in. My heart is so cold and so filled with hate of men that I cannot even say the name of Jesus, the Jesus who rapes and punishes. Can you see, daddy, from where you are, that the only way I could survive was by dissociation and developing "Multiples" to handle the insanity? Can you see the hopelessness that comes out every Wednesday, the wanting to die and begging to die to stop the pain? Do you know of the depth of the inability to know of touch, daddy? My body is so frozen that I cannot let in the touch of a human being even though my heart longs for it. Yes, I have a wonderful husband and he is patient and waits for me to open up that cold heart but it may never happen. My children have been waiting for me too, daddy, waiting for me to realize how much they love me. As adults they know and have always known of my doubt of being loveable and they wait for me to lift this cold heart and accept their love. You see, daddy, God has protected them in spite of my cold heart and in spite of your abuse. As I continue to see Don each week, there's that spark of hope that I can someday heal and integrate. There are some weeks, however, that I experience no hope and slide into an abyss that the children are asking me to feel so that they may integrate.

The ironic part of all of this, daddy, is that Abba (that's the Hebrew word for Father, daddy) has asked me to work to open the hearts of my patients so that He may enter and heal them (the meditation I had a few years ago in which Abba came to me). If you can, daddy, will you pray that my cold heart will be opened someday as well. One last question, did you make mommy sick too or was she already sick?

Mommy, what happened to you? Why did you hate me so much? Why did you tell me so often that I was "evil and going to hell" for what I have done to you? Was it you or auntie that put me in that box and tried to bury me? Who was it, mommy? What made you so sick that you were in mental institutions so much? Why was I the one given away, mommy? And when I did come

Journal Writings Prior to Mary's Visitation

home, why did you tell me you had to clean my vagina out because I was so evil? Why did you tell me you needed to kill my babies, mommy? Why do the children insist there were abortions?

Lastly, mommy, why did I have to live at the orphanage for a while? Did both of you not want me?

August 3, 2012

I researched Paregoric and found it to be an opiate based drug which is rarely used today (in its pure form) but is still used to aid newborn babies who are addicted to heroin. Today a prescription is needed but in the late Forties and Fifties it was readily available. I remember my father coming home with a few large bottles at a time (for his bad stomach problems).

More pieces of my puzzle are coming together. For the last three weeks I have been on a medication called Tramadol. Tramadol is an opiate based drug just like Paregoric. Taking the Tramadol triggered the same physiological response as when I was given Paregoric, thus bringing up the memories of being sexually abused by my father and his giving me over to other men as well.

I have been forced to take Tramadol for pain while awaiting surgery (which is finally scheduled for August 10th). The process of setting up the surgery has been slow-going because of two issues.

Journal Writings Prior to Mary's Visitation

Testing has not been able to determine if I do in fact have ovarian cancer or "something else." Blood work cannot confirm the presence of ovarian cancer cells but on imaging there is a large fluid-filled mass. So exploratory surgery is necessary. Because of the complicating factors, there needs to be two surgeons; a general surgeon in case there needs to be removal of internal organs and my OBGYN in case it involves the ovaries. Setting up a time when both my doctors can do the surgery is the other complicating factor.

So I wait. All I can do is pace and pace and pray. I pace in between patients and pace in the evening and all the while praying. I developed compassion for people who are stricken with such fear and panic. You need to try to act normal and all the while you feel like you are going insane. I can't stop the Tramadol because without it the pain is intense, but taking it brings up such painful memories of the abuse. And to add insult to injury, the upcoming surgery is bringing up the panic of not being in control and being given over to "other men."

August 8, 2012
Dream Last Night

The Blessed Virgin came to me in my dream and said she was going to be at the surgery with the Holy Family. She assured me all will be well. It was a comforting dream, but I'm more worried about the thought of being naked in front of strangers. No matter how often I tell myself it is irrational, it does not matter. The alter children have made themselves known. This surgery is no different than the rapes and torture. They are letting me know the pain they suffered at the hands of their abusers. Their feelings and pain are mine right now. So I enter the time travel at "warp" speed. In an instant, I am back there with them, watching the "men" who hurt me. Only the sound of my office door opening brings me back to this time space. It is the sound of a patient coming in. This hour will be free from the painful past that the children carry. I am so grateful for my patients. So are the children. We all get a much needed rest.

Journal Writings Prior to Mary's Visitation

August 10, 2012
Surgery Day, 6 am

My doctors came in and explained that there could be the need to remove part of my intestines or even worse and that "It was a mess in there." Again, I was not so frightened about that as much as the fear of being alone and naked without anyone to protect me.

When I woke, there was no one around. I felt to see how many holes there were in my belly. Only three small holes which meant there was no radical surgery. Oh thank God. I will be able to get back to my patients sooner rather than later.

I was taken to a recovery room where my patient husband was waiting. He explained it was a cyst filled with fluid that was the size of a large "water balloon." I was going home and will be OK. No ovarian cancer. I later learned that this type of cyst is a rare occurrence, so rare as a matter of fact, that it is a "freak of nature." My case was later presented at the hospital's case conference. My doctor told me, "Janine, you never want to be a freak of nature or presented at a case conference and you were both." She expressed how lucky I was that it turned out all right. It often does not end well. I got to go home and I was such a happy clam, happy and grateful to God. I could now go on with my life as normal or so I thought.

That night I dreamt I was being "commissioned" to write a book and the word "HOME" needed to be in it.

First Meetings with the Blessed Virgin

October 5, 2012, 2am

I woke and was very dizzy. So dizzy, as a matter of fact, I was afraid I would not make the plane to Chicago in two hours. I heard a voice that said, **Bless yourself with the holy water and get into the child pose. I am the Blessed Virgin. Don's story is true and accurate. I clothed you in my protective cloak and kept you alive so that I could get you to this day. On this day I give you back the children** (The Blessed Mother is referring to the alter children, some of which had not fully integrated). I became frightened and asked her not to leave me and she said, *I will be with you always. I will teach you to love as I love all my children.* It was then that I became aware of how it must have been for her to say "yes" to God and carry the Son of Man. She said to me, **Be it done unto me according to your word, oh my Lord.** She instructed me to say it also. After I repeated her words, she said, **Continue to work to "open hearts" just as Abba has instructed, so that He can enter an open heart.** She added, *Keep an open mind to whatever lies ahead. Go and be healthy.* I had no more episodes of dizziness.

Janine Lariviere Coming Home to the Mother

The Orphanage

First Meetings with the Blessed Virgin

October 8, 2012

I began a walking meditation and heard Mary's voice say, *Go get the picture, the one you drew in pencil a few years ago.* I pulled it out and she asked that I go across the street to the drug store and get a frame for it. I asked if there was time as I had a patient in an hour and, if there wasn't a frame there, it would be too far to go to Wall-Mart. Her voice was persistent. I said "OK Mother, if this is a pilgrimage, I am up for it but I never saw frames in this drug store." I got there and went down every aisle and I asked Mother if this was a test to see if I would go on a pilgrimage for her. As I headed out of the store, there at the end cap was a set of frames. I was told at the checkout that this frame had just arrived.

I returned to work and framed her picture and felt her love for me. I meditated again and became aware that the picture I drew of her was the age she had said yes to God's angels. She told me to show it to Don.

October 13, 2012

We began watching my grandson's football game via the computer and I asked Mary to be with me as it was just a game and yet it felt so important. I heard what I felt was her voice saying, ***They will win.*** I began to panic as I was so sure it wasn't her. "Mother Mary, please teach me to know your voice," I said. I heard it again, ***They will win. I tell you this so you will trust that I am with you always.*** "I asked, Will you make them win?" She said, ***No, I can see ahead.*** I was so panicked that all I could do was pray over and over again. "Lord, be it done unto me according to your word." Over and over again I heard, ***I am with you and I do this so you will trust that I am with you.*** My grandson's team was winning with two minutes left and was able to hold the opposing team on their final drive.

Later, as I was sitting, I heard Mother Mary's voice say, ***I will heal you and you will smell the roses and know that you are totally healed.*** I felt she meant my stomach problems will be healed. Then I heard her say, ***Go make some popcorn for you and the children.*** I said "Mother Mary, I have no popcorn. I looked a few days ago and there was none." She repeated that I go and make popcorn. I said, "OK, but if there is no popcorn then please teach me to be able to discern your voice from the noise." Right there in the cabinet was a jar of popcorn and it was in the open. I don't know how I could have missed it. So I made the popcorn and blessed her for loving me so much. After we ate the popcorn, I

First Meetings with the Blessed Virgin

asked the Blessed Mother how I discern her voice. She said, **You will know me by the peace I bring.** She said if I am afraid I have her permission to wait until I feel the peace that goes beyond all understanding. That will allow me to discern her voice. It was then that I felt the peace again and she said, **Get a pen as we need to name the children. Don is right; there are four of them.** So we named them Sarah (Sarah that Don and I know), Rachel, Jane and Bethany.

The Grotto

Integration of alters with the help of Our Lady

October 15, 2012

I sat at work after lunch, closed the lights and waited to see if Mother would come to me. I felt that peace again and heard her voice. She asked me if I knew how old Sarah was and I said nine and she said yes. Then she asked how old I felt Bethany was and I said an infant and she said yes. Then how old was Rachel and I said a fetus and she said yes, I was right. Lastly, how old was Jane and again I heard my heart say a fetus and she said yes. She explained there were two fetuses and two children. She said she is now freeing Rachel and Jane (the fetuses) so that they can be taken up with the angels and archangels, to be nurtured and grow. I feared that the story the alter personalities had told might be true. My father (or whoever) had gotten me pregnant and my mother had aborted them. I did not feel the fear, only expressed it to Mary without words. Without words she let me know that I had given life to two fetuses and she was letting them enter into life everlasting. Again without words she heard my pain that she had waited all these years before freeing them. She said, *In God's time it is but an instant.* She said that she gave life to the other two children and that they are not alters. They are in fact two entities which she gave birth to in order that they not only would protect me but also because of their bravery would enjoy everlasting life outside of me. I asked again through my heart and without words how she could do that and she said, *I am the mother of God, I can do anything.* After they finish protecting me, they will enter heaven and I will be healed and smell the roses. So, not only my digestive issues will be healed but also my heart will be healed. Then we sat in peace in the Garden and I felt the fetuses leave.

    She told me not to fear. A person need only open his or her heart for but an instant and in that instant they will know the Son of Man (albeit on an unconscious level). They may close their heart again on this earth but will be given a second chance to choose Jesus in the next. It's then that they will recall the love of Jesus and choose the Savior. We need to pray for the closed hearted for they may say no at the second chance. Mother knew of my terrible fear that, because I work with those of no faith, they may not enter the

Integration of alters with the help of Our Lady

Kingdom. Her words made me understand the true meaning of my meditation in which Abba had instructed me to work towards opening up hearts.

I asked her if she would come back in an hour after my next session and she said yes. When I came back, she instructed me to go and get ice cream with the children. I am right next door to Dairy Queen and so I did. I am lactose intolerant and yet I suffered no ill effects.

October 18, 2012

I meditated and heard Mary tell me to hold the two children that are left. She has fought to save me and I am hers. She told me go and research Santeria. It will be important.

I began my web search with "Wikipedia" and began to feel sick as I read of the Santeria cult that hid behind the Roman Catholic saints and sacrificed animals in a ritual. The Roman Catholic Church felt they were bringing Christianity to the slaves they took. But rather than transform their religion, it forced them to devise a way to keep their ritualistic behaviors. Oh Dear God, could the children be right? Could they have witnessed the sacrifice of animals? I was too sick to go any further.

Integration of alters with the help of Our Lady

4:00 pm

I was able to meditate again. This time I went deeply into the Garden with Mary. I felt my body move away and I felt like I didn't need to breathe. I didn't feel my breath. I didn't feel my body. Mary asked me if I could see the flowers in the Garden and I said no. She said, **Come deeper into the Garden and soon you will. You need to look through your heart and not your eyes.** I asked her if I was dissociating and she said no. I wouldn't be able to hear her if I was dissociating. She said she was pleased that I had researched the Santeria and now she would explain. Sarah was holding the physical pain of the rapes while Bethany held the pain of the Santeria. Bethany had been sacrificed to the Santeria and been given to the devil. I was not to fear because there is no evil in her. She further explained that she made her a separate entity precisely because if she were an alter personality there would be need for exorcism. I am to tell Don not to fear. As the pain comes out from Bethany, he is to assure me that I am not of the devil. She is a separate entity so that I may know the true nature of God and his love for me. Mother said, **He sanctioned me to care for you.** I asked why, "I am but a sinner." She didn't answer but her love for me was so certain at that point. I began to feel the words of the devil and she said it is not the devil. It is the voices of the Santeria who wanted to sacrifice me to the devil. I never felt fear, just some confusion. Then she asked, **Are you ready to feel the pain from Bethany.** I said "Yes, Mother, you know I am. I have dedicated myself to you." She said, **I need to have you say yes.** I began to feel pain in my vagina and heard the screams. She said again, **Do not be afraid for I have already saved you.** Then I said, "I need to write this down," and she said, **Yes.** I opened my eyes and was surprised that I could see her picture and still had no breath or body. I see my handwriting but still cannot feel my breathing. I had asked her if Don's friend Dave needed to know. She said, **Yes, Don will need help as well.** As I finish this, I still cannot feel my breathing. It is so peaceful. I feel like I am floating. Thank you, Mary, for your love and bringing me into the light of God's salvation. I am so honored. I will spend the rest of my life blessing you. When I can, I will go to the place where I believed it all happened.

Integration of alters with the help of Our Lady

October 30, 2012

Mother Mary, you have asked me to write this down. Please help me to remember what happened last Thursday and last Friday so that I may honor your words. Let them be your words again. Help me to not miss anything.

I tried to meditate this morning and tears came. Mother asked me to write down what happened and she will be with me in the Garden later.

Last Thursday night (October 24th) at 10pm, I felt the need to go lie on the couch rather than stay in bed. I had set the alarm for two am because of our trip to Chicago. I began to feel a pull from my body and I heard the Blessed Virgin ask, **Are you willing to stay awake all night.** I remember feeling scared and saying, "I need sleep but your will be done." She then asked, **Would you stay up in order to be healed.** I said, "Yes." I fell into my body at a deep level, a cellular level. I felt my lower belly burn and it burned for almost the whole four hours. I remember being in my body at such a deep level that even a gas bubble felt like the roar of thunder. My belly burned and burned and I knew I should be feeling intense pain and I should be sweating, but neither happened. Instead, it felt glorious to be giving my body over to her as she saw fit. The hours flew by and all of a sudden I saw the most beautiful tree that was the color of the rainbow, plus more intense than any ordinary rainbow. I thanked her for letting me see through my heart for the first time. I also saw faces, yet not faces as we know them. It was just a flash. I asked what had happened and she said it would be revealed. I asked myself all day what had happened but couldn't figure it out, only that each moment of those four hours was miraculous.

On Friday, we were still in Chicago and I got up and went into the shower. I heard Mother's voice and I tested to see if it was coming from my heart or my head . I felt sure it was from my heart. I also felt the peace that she said would discern her voice. I heard her say, **Check your rectum. I have healed your hemorrhoid as well as the fissures near your anus.** I felt and went inside my rectum and the large hemorrhoid was gone. I had never noticed fissures so I don't know about any changes, but I do know my hemorrhoid was gone. She told me it needed to be healed in order that a deep healing of my internal organs can happen. I began to bless her and she said that Kublai Khan was now an archangel because he opened his heart to God. I thought, "OK, Mother, I will be able to check that

Integration of alters with the help of Our Lady

out when I am with you." She also said that Joseph (not the real name) was now healed of his temper tantrums (Joseph is a young man with Down's Syndrome whom we met at a tailgating party just before my grandson's football game, so I have no way of knowing about him). The last thing she said was she would be helping me to experience an orgasm that would truly be mystical. About an hour later my daughter sent me a video of Joseph and he was announcing "Game Day." How truly remarkable as we both don't know him well and she thought to send it to me. I felt it was no coincidence.

November 6, 2012

The thoughts of Joseph keep coming into my mind, so I texted my daughter about him. I told her I had a dream about Joseph (I was afraid to say I hear the Blessed Mother's voice) and asked her to keep her ears open to Joseph's possible tantrums. She said she would.

Integration of alters with the help of Our Lady

November 9, 2012

I was driving back to work and knew I had a few hours, so I drove to my home town to see the "bathtub virgin." I began to pray that it would not have a shelf and I don't know why. When I arrived, it was not a bathtub virgin but a two story grotto with a statue of the Blessed Virgin in it. I pulled in and went down the long driveway to the grotto and looked for someone to give me permission to be there. There appeared to be no one there. I saw a stone shelf in the grotto. I took a few pictures and looked around. There was a small shed on the side of the driveway where I used to cross into the yard from my aunt's house. There was a stone statue of St. Francis (the patron saint of animals) facing the shed, so its back was to the driveway. Underneath the saint was a circle of stone and it looked like a burial site (of the animals). I don't know why I thought that but I did and it appeared weird that it faced the building and not the driveway. I walked back to the grotto and noticed the blue angel and felt sick inside. So I left.

When I got back to work, I looked at the pictures I had taken, especially the statue of the Blessed Virgin. It was of the young Virgin Mary on the same idea as my drawing. The blue angel appears to be a child with breasts and it haunts me.   I pray for the courage to call the owners of the grotto and get permission to go back as well as to talk to someone about the grotto.

Integration of alters with the help of Our Lady

November 14, 2012

My session with Don brought out the perversions that happened at the Grotto. Sarah felt the pain of the animal sacrifices as well as the physical abuse and the devil worship. I felt sick all day.

November 15, 2012
Dream last night

I was in a church (a church in the town I was raised). I was in the back at the side pew and it was time for Communion. There was a Eucharistic Minister giving out Communion in the back aisle but we were being directed to go to the altar. I was carrying a lot of bags and had to put them on one arm in order to receive. I went to receive and the priest sat down and refused to give me Communion. The young woman went to give me Communion and I said, "I will come back later." I was hurt and confused. As I headed back, a young man said to me, "do you know who stole your money?" I said yes, "It was the priest. He was the only one who had the time to do it."

Integration of alters with the help of Our Lady

November 15, 2012

I spoke with Don and I explained that the church in the dream was a closed church to all but the few who came from Italy. He felt that it represented the out-of-tradition of the church (the Santeria) and went on to say the priest stole the knowledge.

November 16, 2012

The Mother spoke to me on the way to work and I asked her to take away the noise. She said she already has and that she will explain the dream (I felt that beautiful peace again). Don was right; the church represents the Santeria. I am being taken to the altar of the Santeria and I am carrying news, the covenant, and trusts in the bag. The news is my need to research and educate myself in matters like my belly pain, the Santeria and knowledge of the Blessed Virgin. The covenant is the covenant with Abba. The trusts (like family trusts) are the promises passed down from her to me and my generations like the promise that she will bless them and give them everlasting life because I have said yes to her.

She then said that the priest is the priestess meaning her (the Blessed Virgin) who refused to let me be in communion with them (the Santeria). She said it was she who stole or took the knowledge of it and that I was asked by the Holy Spirit if I knew who took it. I knew because she had told me that before (that she held the story

Integration of alters with the help of Our Lady

in both Bethany and Sarah in order to have kept me from going insane). Then she said the dream did not say, "He was the only one who had the time." The dream said ,"He was the only one who could have stolen the money," meaning the Mother is the only one who could have taken the knowledge from me.

Then she spoke in that beautiful knowing deep inside of me and she said, *I love you and walled you off from all that knowledge until now so that you could survive. That is why you have felt so isolated and negated all your life. You lived a life of self absorption because it was your only world. I am sorry that you felt so isolated but what we have now will more than make up for it. The first Fridays and first Saturdays that you did were no accident. I led you to the church so that those prayers, even though you didn't realize it, were an offering to save the people of the Santeria so that they may know the true God. It was no accident that you felt the need to do them for me. Father Barrette* (The Blessed Virgin is referring to our parish priest who would come for home visits on occasion) *would come to the house on Carnation Street and would pray for you, although unknowing how those prayers would help. Not all priests are of the devil, Janine, just a few of those that hurt you. Yes, the Santeria had some priests but they were self-entitled priests, not those ordained. A child has no way of knowing that. Who they or the others were does not matter, just that you will save nations from the torture of not knowing God at the second chance. For that the Father is grateful.*

I love you despite all your faults. The world does not see the saint in you but I do, my child. Write this as I dictate so that the generations may hear and be healed. I am the Blessed Virgin Mary and I entrust you with a new name of Bernadette (it is the name I will call you by...Janine of the sisterhood of Bernadette) for you have researched her and know that she is one of my followers of the Rosary. She has set nations free with her prayers and suffering as well. I do not ask more than you can bear. I will give you insights into the world of the Father because of your trust in me. Write as I dictate and be sure to have both pictures of me open. One is the faithful drawing that you and Sarah (one of the alter personalities that had not yet integrated) *drew and the other is the one of the grotto. There is blood there but it is the blood of my Father that has saved them and you. Pray for those who have perished there for they did not understand my Father's love, only his anger and rage at those who were so perverted. My Father does not act in anger, only love. Just as Jesus was angry that some men perverted the synagogue, He is angry that people have perverted the grotto. He feels anger but never acts on it like humans do. He does not punish his children. He only wants them to return to him. I tell you again He does not punish. It is his love*

Integration of alters with the help of Our Lady

that brings people to the altar. Jesus was crucified and what his people forget is that He has risen. Where the cross was, there now stands a beautiful tree in all its blossoms (just as Abba showed you when he took you to the cross). We need to remember He died for us but it is equally important that we know He is risen and alive in all of us. He wants us to live with the knowledge that He lives and loves and so wants all of his children to have eternity with Him. I am the guide to the light of his love. How tragic and painful his eyes are when someone does not chose Him at the second chance. Pray for all souls who do not know of Him. Even a glimpse of Him in an open moment is enough to choose Him at the second chance. Go now, child, and do your work. Come back often for I will be your guide.

Thank you so much, Mother. My tears are one of gratitude for your love and kindness to me. The weekly pain in the sacred room with Don now has meaning and for that I am truly grateful. I am also truly grateful for your love for me especially right now. I am so humbled at your ability to love so much and I pray that all souls can know you as I do right now.

Where Mother uses Janine's hands

Mother Explains the Role of Sin, Shaping and the Ego

November 16, 2012, 2:16 pm

Mother, what is it you direct me to write about?

The world is a sad place. Bring joy and happiness not gloom and doom. My Father wishes the world to find joy in his love. Death is but a pathway back to me but this earth life is meant to have joy. My way is light hearted and joyous as you are learning. Bring your joy and light heartedness into those you meet and it will stretch around the globe. God says my way is the way of truth and light, he who follows me will know life everlasting. My Father does not ask that you stop finding joy in living, but just the opposite. Find joy in your cup of coffee. Find joy in your children. Be the "heart light" for others.

The smile you drew is the smile I wish to impart to the world.

The picture at the grotto (The Blessed Virgin is referencing a picture I took of the statue at the grotto) *is not who I am. It is one of pain that comes out of sin, but it is not who I am. I am the Blessed Virgin who said yes to the angels of God and, as confusing as it was, it was a labor of joy. How could God have chosen me, a sinner, to change the world? And so, my child, you say how could I have chosen you. For the same reason because you have said yes. All those years ago, when I asked you if you were ready to feel the pain, you said yes; if it will save others, and you said yes. Yes, my child, it was I who asked you to feel the pain so that others may live. Bless the children and bless you for allowing the children to tell their story, for in doing that you have released so many others of the bondage of sin.*

Now to address sin: It matters not what you call it. Your words are shaping. My words are the sins of our fathers; they are the sins that we need to become conscious of in order to stop the sins from passing down further. It is also what you call original sin. It does not negate Adam and Eve's sin of disobedience, it expands on it. For that was the first sin to be passed down through the generations. It is that passing down of the sins of past generations that are evil; for a child born has no sin of its own. It has the sins of all the previous generations. I am the Mother of God and I have the love of all children in my heart. You are all

Mother Explains the Role of Sin, Shaping and the Ego

children of God and all need to see the world as one of changing the unconscious things we learn. What you call the unspoken rules. You have been given a beautiful gift and you reach many people with your words of "not placing blame." As you tell God's children that come to you...It is not about blame, it is about seeing the truth, the truth of shaping. The truth is that you come from a sinful past and it needs the light of the truth brought in. Even the greatest of sinners can find Jesus when they see their shaping in a loving and non-judgmental light. Too many people are taught to be loyal to their ancestors and have a misconception about that. It is not sinful or disloyal to look at your past. It is the truth that we must seek. Go and love as I love.

November 17, 2012

Mother, what is it you need me to write today?

Do not fear, my child, I am with you. I give you my love and attention and respect for your attempts to be perfect as I am perfect. Perfection comes only in the afterlife with God but you try hard. Come with me into the Garden and feel the love of all the generations who are in the Garden with Jesus and the Holy Trinity. God so loved the world He gave his only Son up for execution. He so loved the world that He sent the Holy Spirit so that man can know Him from the inside, if only man would look inside to hear the voice of the Holy Spirit. The Holy Spirit is one of guidance and such love as you know. The Spirit never condemns but guides in the most loving of ways. Ego loses its power when we are in the company of the Holy Spirit. Do not fear your ego for it has no power here. The ego does not want you to believe because it fears not being in control. Giving up control is a very frightening thing for most people, but as you are learning, it is not at all giving up

Mother Explains the Role of Sin, Shaping and the Ego

control, it is choosing. You have chosen to come here and ask if I want you to write and ego wants you to believe that I do not exist. It is so afraid to risk knowing me or Jesus or the Holy Spirit because of that innate fear of being so bad and not being worthy.

How do I change that, Mother?

You change that by giving it to me. I am the source of the light because I am the Mother of God Who is the Light. When you turn it over to me or Jesus or the Holy Spirit, it gives the power and energy to the heavens to move whatever mountains need to be moved in order to bring souls to the light.

Go now and light up your world.

Thank you, Mother.

November 19, 2012

What is it you want me to write, Mother?

Tell of the pain you have suffered. Tell of all the pain from Saturday.

There is a pain in my heart that all men are driven by the penis, that they care not for a woman but only for the relief of their sexual desires. I asked you if it was true and you gave no answer, but I saw the clear picture of a hooded priest. I am grateful that you told me it was not an ordained priest and then you told me to read and hear what I wrote about looking at the truth of our past. Please give me peace, Mother, so that this terrible fear goes away.

I promise you, child, there will be peace in your heart from following me. So now continue to write because the most important thing is to bring souls to God. So as you write, remember that ego has no home here, only my words in your heart, Janine. The men who raped and battered you were men of

Mother Explains the Role of Sin, Shaping and the Ego

an evil spirit, that of the Santeria. The face you saw was one of them. He wore a Jewish robe and expressed himself as a Jewish God and called himself "Abba." Yes, that is where you first heard the name, but Abba protected you. Please do not fear using Abba's name for it was those who perverted the name that hurt you, not the true Abba. What happened Saturday was that I allowed you to see the face of the self proclaimed Abba who used rituals to hurt children. Many children were hurt when he spread the word that they needed to be sacrificed in a sexual ritual and given over to the devil to save them and others. It was based on the notion that children do not remember and so any pain and memory will be forgotten.

So, feel your feelings right now and be angry and sad for all the children who were abused. God has blessed the children and sanctioned me to help you to tell the truth and, as God sees fit, it will be exposed. For the souls of these men need to be redeemed and the Father wishes them to enter the gates of heaven. They have asked forgiveness and they work with angels and Archangels to free those children who are still in so much pain that they hide from God because they were told they are evil. Beverly is one such child. She is now at peace with God and wishes to bring peace to you and the other children.

There is one more thing I need of you, my dear sweet child.

Pray the Rosary daily for the salvation of souls, those whose hearts are so closed only prayer and grace will open them.

Yes, Mother

A Special Blessing From the Father

November 20, 2012

Mother has directed me to write.

Today I give you a special gift. The Father has given you a special blessing. One of love and gratitude that you continue to choose Mary, the Mother of God who is the one and only Blessed Virgin to not have suffered original sin. Also, I give you the beginning of your life back. I have given you back the beauty of your virginity for it was taken away at such a young age and without your willingness. You have been forgiven the sin of lust from those who lusted after you. Their lust blemished your beautiful gift of virginity that you can now share with Ed. You will be able to begin anew and feel the beautiful virgin within you and make the choice to give it to him. You never felt pure enough to even be married and I know that in order to be truly married to Ed that needs to heal. So hear my words again, you have been forgiven and redeemed for the lust of other men. It is not because you need to be forgiven for their sins but your prayers for them have redeemed them from their lust and that forgiveness comes back to you in the form of grace. The Blessed Mother has shown you that it is only prayers and her grace that truly heals. Humans cannot heal themselves for there are too many confounding factors that mess up the researchers. It is a bad road to go down alone without the grace of God. These are all the things the Mother has shared with you today in that instant of being in her company. She speaks to you as fast as you can conjure up the questions.

More on the Santeria

November 26, 2012

Mother, what is it you wish me to write?

My heart is an open heart, a heart that aches to have all of God's children know Him. Your prayers are being heard. My child, stop being afraid, you are not of the Santeria. You are not of the devil. The men in robes have defiled your body and that of other children. I know how much you struggle with worry and fear that my voice is of the evil one but the fruits of my voice will be seen. Trust in my wisdom for you cannot have the insights on your own. The God of your father was one of the false gods that you were given. Please trust my voice. Hear me, child, for I was the one who plucked you out of the many who were hurt and damaged. This is your task, child, to now feel all their pain, for it is in feeling all the pain that they will be free as well. Just as Sarah and

Bethany hold your pain, you also hold the pain of those who died in the face of the Santeria. Janine, this goes far beyond your imagination. No, you have no memory of it. It would have killed you, so I hold the memory. Trust that all the pain that has come out of your body in twenty years is true and real. Week after week all that has been held in your body cannot be made up, even though you want it to be. God the Father has willed that all that horrible pain can be released through your body so that all of those of the Santeria can be healed. Please love yourself for you are not of the Santeria. You are a child of God and He has blessed you. Go now and fear not. The Lord be with you and yours. Blessed be the name of God and of the Blessed Virgin and her holy name. God true God of true God, begotten not made of one in Being with the Father, the Son and the Holy Spirit. Go now and do your work. Know that God and I are with you, for it is in loving my children that you give back to the Father for all his blessings on you. Fear not your words because, as Abba has told you, it is of the Holy Spirit that your words are his words and that He heals through your words. Remember your covenant with God. Remember also that the devil no longer has control. You have been redeemed by my love and my covenant.

More on the Santeria

November 29, 2012

Mother, bless my hands. What is it you wish me to write?

The Santeria was a worldwide cult that the Father has been hurt and shamed by (yes the Father feels all human feelings) for these people used the saints as a front to do their evil work. Not all Santeria used the devil as their worship, but there was a cult who did and used sexuality as the way to honor the devil. It was a terrible cult that went to extremes to offer alms to the evil one. It was sex that drove these men and some women to use devil worship. It is in God's time that it will be revealed. It is not of your ability to prove my words but God will in his time. The pain you feel is one of fear and the pain of sexual intercourse by evil men. They did evil to children and animals to gain sexual satisfaction. They did it in the name of a god they called Abba. Your father and others need to be healed and are asking for your prayers and your courage right now. I know your fear and your pain. The hopelessness you carry right now is that of not just your pain but the pain of all that you witnessed at the hands of these men. You must carry it for now, Janine, for you have been chosen and you have said yes. I am with you in all this pain. You do not need to do anything more than to understand the pain in your head, bosom, genitals and belly area is of the past and the devil worship. It will get better.

Mother, do I cancel my appointment with the allergist?

No, go so that others can be witness to my healing, for I shall make you a bearer of God's healing powers that go beyond the medical world. God has so loved you, child, that he brought witness to you in the name of Don. Be not afraid for your pain is not of self doing but one in which the Father wishes to heal through you. Bear your pain with love and dignity. Bring your head up and not down for you have done nothing wrong. I have given you the edict on how to eat. Now your body will be able to handle the pain and won't be confused with what your doctor has called IBS. There is a difference between the two. I shall teach you. Eat as I have shown you. I am with you and will help you. Do not be afraid. The pain will not overtake you and you will be able to continue to bear witness to the pain of others. It is the bearing of this pain that makes you understand the pain of others in a way that all may not understand. It is the same pain the Father feels when He cannot reach others. It is the pain of

More on the Santeria

wanting the whole world to know the joy of God's love. All you need do is witness the pain of others one soul at a time as God brings them to you and continue to pray for all souls that they may know the true God.

So tell me, child, what have you learned.

That as I trust you and write, my heart becomes lighter and the evil that I fear holds me is gone. You have lifted me to a new plane and for that I am grateful. You showed me that bearing the pain in the name of you and Jesus is not a pain of being bad or evil, but the pain that I have been chosen to bear and I bear it with love for you and God. So, I write it again to be sure and say it in another way. I have done nothing wrong to deserve this pain and no amount of self chastising will change it. I give it all to you with love. Help me to be the therapist I need to be.

I will be with you and help you for you speak my words. You are bearing witness to the pain of others. Go and know that you are loved and I wish you to write. It is in the writing that all becomes clear and so please stop being so afraid that evil will infiltrate the writing. I promise you that I will not allow any evil to come from your hands as you write. Janine of the Sisterhood of Bernadette, that name has been given to you so that you can be connected to another who has the passion to help souls reach God.

A depiction of Bernadette at Lourdes

More on the Santeria

November 30, 2012

Blessed Mother, bless my hands. What is it you wish of me today?

Write as I dictate. Your heart is open to my words and I am pleased that you now know my voice above the noise. I wish you to visit the grotto and pray there for all the lost souls. I will guide your way when the time is right. Do not fear, I will show you the way. Bring Don or Pamela with you. They both carry the Holy Spirit that will be a guide for you as well as eyes for you. There are things they can see that you cannot. Yes, call the phone number for the people who own the grotto and talk to whoever answers the phone.

I followed your call, Mother, and thank you for the courage to call the owners of the grotto. The woman has given me permission to go any time. She remembered my aunt and uncle. She spoke of her family who live on the same land as she. She told me her name and said she remembered me from my aunt and the time I spent there. Oh my God, she remembered me. She told me about my cousin who lives in my aunt's house still today. You know my heart, Mother, and it is with love that I have done this, but it is also so painful.

Fear not, child, you have done as I have asked and I will bless the efforts. It is difficult, I know, but I have given you the courage. Now bear witness to my word. The love of God follows you and will bring fruit to your loving efforts. There are children who will see the light of God's power and majesty because of your efforts and Don's and Pamela's. Trust her for she is of God as well. She has known of Him since childhood and heard his voice as well. She has had to go through such addiction and pain so that she can bear witness to you in your journey. Let her light and yours and Don's shine, for your lights shine the way to my Father.

Child, please believe in me for I will never forsake you. You are so fearful because you have been forsaken by those who were responsible for you. I have not asked you to do anything that will bring down the wrath of God on you. Those were the false gods of the Santeria, not the Father of my Son. Bring your fear to the Cross and it will bring you to the risen Christ. I had to watch Him die and that pain has been released so that I could know him as the Son of the Creator. So I promise you, you shall know the Creator as I know Him, that of love, love that goes beyond human

More on the Santeria

awareness. I shall never leave you. Feel my love and go now for I have taken the fear away and you can move on to seeing the souls God will bring to you tonight. Go in love and shine his light for Him.

Janine at Two at auntie's

God's Plan for all His Children

December 01, 2012

Mother, what is it you wish me to write?

My child, I am the light that shines from my Father who wills me to come to you. It is the light of salvation that works through you and others with open hearts. It is the heart that finds Jesus and the light. The heart knows whence it came from on a very deep level even before conception. God's heart is ever expanding. He creates a child even before conception and pours his heart into that child. The heart from God's initial and loving asking for a child to be born has been given his heart. So, whether a child is born into the world or not matters little (in regards to the soul) for each child that God wills into life will find its place. The world may find this a difficult matter but there are some children who were not meant to be born. They were meant to live a life with the angels right from the start. Children unborn, and yes the fetuses, are given a place in God's kingdom; so blessed are those who suffer the loss of a child. They have such pain and yet have given another person for God to love. For that child, there is a special place in God's plan because they are absolved of original sin. Child, do not fear, I have told you there is no blasphemy here. It is God's light that shines from me to you and I have told you before these insights cannot come from your mind. Your mind cannot fathom the ways of God to this degree. But it is God's hope that someday those who have had such losses will be grateful to God for they shall know their children in the new world.

Mother, I am but your servant; you grace me so much. I am not worthy of these insights. Thank you and I will do your will as you see fit.

I have told you my will. You are to visit the grotto and it will be difficult but it will free many souls. I will find the time for you when the time is right.

The fetuses of your aunt were buried at the grotto, Janine. That is why you never found their graves. She had such angst at the loss of those twins that she began to hate you because she felt it was the second twin who killed the first in her body. You were the second twin. It is why she hated you and she taught your mother to hate you as well, for your mother was accused of being

God's Plan for all His Children

with your uncle. If you have DNA done, you will find that your uncle is your father, but you do not need to do that for it will not matter. I tell you this for your information and I will let you know what to do with this information at a later time. For now understand that it is because of the fetuses that I tell you this story. They are alive and well in God's kingdom and they all work for the healing of all those souls who suffer from the Santeria.

Now to the topic of God's plan. God loves all his children and He has many rooms in his house. Souls have a special place in God's house right from the beginning of God's plan, so even before conception God has made a plan for them. God waits to place that child in a special way in a special family with all that is needed to heal the family from past generations of shaping. Because of choice, however, God's plan is often misunderstood and misused. That is why the angels and archangels work to bring all of my lost sheep home.

It is confusing for you, I know, for the Father speaks through me and sometimes it is his words as well. Just write and it will become clear later. God's plan was to have his children love and share the heart of his gentleness and caring, but because of the original sin it became clouded with anger, fear, lust and sadness. It is truly not the fault of the generations. Because of shaping we absorb the good and bad of previous generations. We need more prayer and love, not chastising. Love opens the heart and allows the heart to see the shaping. Have you not noticed that the less you preach and the more you enter their painful world, that the more my loving heart can do the work? A closed heart only sees your guidance as preaching. An open one sees my Father, for it is in the deepest recesses that they know the Father. You merely need to be the receptacle of my love and let the heart of my heart do the work.

Let me say it again, child. The heart of God's heart is given to each of us even before conception, so on a very innate and deep level each heart knows the Father. The world needs to preach less and listen more to the longings of another's heart. When the longings are allowed to surface, the heart opens and begins to remember God on that deep and innate level. Yes, there is need to teach and an open heart is ready to hear the teachings of God. But be assured even a child who has never learned of God on earth has a knowing deep inside of him because he owns a part of God's heart.

The Way of the Gift

December 03, 2012

Mother spoke to me on the way to work after going back home to look for my notepad. I was in a panic for all this information is on it. I searched the house and got even more panicked. Then I remembered I only need to change the password. So I changed it immediately and, as I did, I heard my notepad ding with an email. There it was on Ed's desk, a place I never leave it. I was so frustrated because I was going to use the time for prayer and meditation with the Blessed Virgin.

As I drove back, Mother spoke to me clearly. She asked me to describe what I was feeling. My heart was so open that I felt it could contain the whole world and Mother said, **It is the gift I bring you, Janine. That is the way of the gift. It can come anywhere** *and you needed to go home. It is not the place you are but the timing of my gifts.* She then asked me to again feel my body and describe it. I had pain in my ears and mouth but my open heart made that pain glorious. Mother said, *Yes, that is the way of my gift.* Now I will know the joy of giving to God all of me and my pain and glory. My heart, as I write, is still so open I am in awe of her love. Mother says the pain in my jaw and mouth is from the Santeria and is beginning to surface, but she wanted me to be fully aware of the difference. It is not the pain of the food allergies but the pain of the santeria. The headache is of the allergies.

The Father wills only good for his children. The giving of yourself is good and not all pain is bad. There is glory when the pain is in the Father's name.

As to the gift of the open heart today, notice how unafraid you were when we talked about telling Ed. You had just panicked at the thought of it and yet now it is not only joyous in your heart but also a possibility. When the time is right, you will have this feeling. You will also have it when it is time to allow Pamela in. Then, if it be God's will, it will expand. For as you now know, I have opened your heart, but there is work in the timing as I have to make sure they are ready to hear. God's ways are powerful and we need only to rest in the comfort of his will to do good.

Blessed be the name of the Father, Son and Holy Spirit.

Mother Speaks of Hate and Hell

December 4, 2012

Mother, you know my heart. What is it you wish me to write about?

Yes, I know your heart is heavy and I am pleased that you are here with me. Write for I will bless your efforts today.

The will of the Father is that your writing be a window into the light of his love. There is so much sadness and pain in the world. My Father only wishes for all to find Him for the beauty of his kingdom goes beyond all understanding and earthly pain and sorrow. Hate originates from lack of trust in the Father. Hate hardens a soul because of felt injustices. Justice is the Father's for He alone can bring what you call justice to be served. I know you love your children. Can you cast them into hell for a perceived injustice? Your numbness is your hurt and anger at all the injustice, but it is only perceived. You have been wounded by people who had a perceived knowledge of a god that is not of God as we know Him. Love is all encompassing and heals all, even those who hurt you. Woundedness begets hate and healing of that woundedness begets love. It is the love of God that heals. Heaven and Earth shall be aware of this mystery all in God's time.

Mother Speaks of Hate and Hell

December 4, 2012
Later in the Day

Mother, do you wish me to write?

Yes, my child. You are beginning to become aware of the awe and majesty that I place into your fingers. I am pleased with your changing attitude. It is in this holy place that I can join you in God's love. The voice you hear is mine loud and clear and the reason you are often left feeling like you are in another world is because you are. The light is with you when you write and it pleases the Father. You have shown through all your fear that you still say yes. It is becoming clear what your fingers need to do. There is always a beautiful place here for you. It is holy ground, Janine, and God has a plan for you. As you know, what you wrote earlier made no sense, it was unreal. Yet, when you go back later, it is of God and his light shines through me. I will bless all that you do. I know you because you are my child. Little did your abusers know that my light was with you from the start. Beautiful child, they could only harm your outer core not your inner core because I protected you. Yes, there will be pain but you will bear it with Don with my help and love. Don said yes so long ago. You need not keep fearing his withdrawal; he has been with me from the start as well. The pain he bears witness to is of utmost importance to the Father. God will bear fruit through both of you. Your nakedness of heart is a joy to the Father, Janine. I bear witness as well, for your yes to God through all these years brings great joy for all the souls you have reached by your yes.

Is there a hell, my Mother?

Child, there is not the hell you perceive. The hell is the saying no to God on the second chance, for these souls will never know the beauty and joy of God's love. It is a hell of sorts. Those who say yes will know his love and forgiveness and will have a place in his kingdom. So pray for all souls because it is hard to fathom eternity without God. Continue to pray the Rosary for lost souls.

Mother Speaks of Hate and Hell

December 5, 2012

Mother of the Grotto and Mother of the most holy Rosary, what is it you wish me to write?

The pain you feel is that of your deepest wound, that of the penis. It's the ultimate hatred of men, for you generalized all those wounds and even learned to hate Jesus because he was a man. That is why you could never use his name until recently. You learned to hate the thought of heaven because they taught you only virgins are allowed in heaven. They defiled you intentionally so that you would be of the devil. Once your virginity was taken, it gave them the excuse to continue to rape you because you were defiled anyway. So, now does it all make sense? You could never strive for heaven because of an unforgivable sin. They taught you that it was hopeless and that is the hopelessness you felt today. I will make it plain for you. They made you feel that there was no hope for heaven, so you gave up and that is why you felt the anger today as well. They took all hope from you. Even before you knew what the word virgin meant, they were penetrating you. They also used the word lost innocence. That is why you got angry at Father Barrett for using the word innocent even at the young age of five. You knew you were not innocent. The total hopelessness and rage comes from the lost innocence and helplessness of feeling you could never get to heaven. That is also what your father felt for he was a part of it all too, Janine. He went from abused to abuser. So now do you understand what he passed down to you through the sick generations? Believe in me for this is the blessing that will set you free. When the rage comes up, ask Don for help to be there and witness the healing power of God. The rage is what you fear most because it was rage that destroyed your innocence.

Continue, my child, for this is the knowledge I impart on you. Your fear has not gone unnoticed but it is the fear of your own rage. Remember what I had you write yesterday about hate. Hate hardens a soul. Yes, you were hurt in the deepest recesses of your body but the hate hardens you only. Do not fear, Father will heal that, but for now know you need to give it to me and the Father. You need to have the courage to express it with Don. It is the way to allow it to be healed. Ask Don to witness the rage with a loving eye. It will not continue to consume you that way.

The Cleansing

December 6, 2012

Mother, I am so sick and in so much pain, it is hard to write.

Yes, child, I know. I will bless your pain. The pain and hurt is so deep and so encompassing that it brings you back to the Santeria."

Bless my hands, Mother, for I don't know if I can go on. Be with me please.

I am with you, child, just write as I dictate. The pain is that of the Santeria and you bear it well. It does not go unnoticed.

I ask you to write not just for yourself but for those whom God wishes to read this. My loving grace is with you. You need to feel this so that you can be cleansed of the anger and hate you have carried. The pain you feel is for those who didn't survive the torture. I need you to bear witness to the pain of those who suffered as you did, Beverly and other children who suffered so much. These men and women got sexual gratification from hurting children and animals but especially children. My Father wants it written. He will give it root when it is time or necessary. There are so many painful stories at the Grotto. That is why you need to go there.

Yes, but what about you, child? I hear your torment and pain and it is so you can understand on that deep level what actually happened. You cannot deny it any longer. The pain you feel is no longer in the hands of Bethany and Sarah. It is now yours, child, and it is tormenting I know, but I am with you and the Father and I bear it with you. Bow your head and be with me........

Call Don and ask him to listen and bear witness.

Now, child, continue. The Father is pleased with your efforts and the pain is now real. So the others need not hold it any more. They are free to be with the Father in his glory for now you can do the work. They are in God's hands now and for that He is joyous. Please understand, child, this does not negate you for your place with Him is cemented.

This is why part of your spirit is at the grotto. I am with you and you will be able to work. I will give you the grace to continue. Trust in me. Each time you allow your spirit to go to the grotto, you will see and hear the pain and torture. However, it is with

The Cleansing

your "yes" that the souls there will be cleansed also. God is with you, child, and so am I.

Again, child, this is why nothing feels solid under your feet right now. You are both in the current world and the past. That is why the Grotto is so much a part of your present today. It will all be healed in God's time.

December 7, 2012

Mother, I am here and in your holy company. What is it you wish of me?

I wish you to be of a pure heart; that is why this is happening at this time. You will be cleansed and purified not only for your sake but for others.

I shall teach you the difference between abuse and the total giving to another that true love is. You had to give without consent and never learned the love of giving from a pure heart. Your heart bears the burden of having to close up so long ago and it is the burden of so many women who know not how to give freely. I shall teach you so you can teach other women. When you are in the throes of confusion and worry about "Is this love or abuse," turn it over to me and let me show you the way. It is not of the will that things change, it is of grace. Ask for my grace and I will move your heart to an understanding. It is the same knowing that you are aware of right now. My words have no meaning yet,

The Cleansing

but they will.

Take time daily to go back and reflect on my words.

December 8, 2012

Mother, what is it you wish me to write today?

The Holy Spirit is alive and well within you. The Father is pleased with the risk you took yesterday. You are teaching Pamela to trust the Holy Spirit deep within her. The Spirit she called Mother yesterday. All is well in her heart because you have validated the Spirit's voice within her. It is just a beginning but she heard my voice call her name. If only the world would know of the voice of my Father deep inside, there would be no pain and sadness and sin. So, my child, teach as I open the opportunities for you. Validate the Spirit as that little, beautiful voice deep inside each human being. Teach your children and grandchildren of the loving voice that always, always uses the language of love and requires no work or payback. It is a gift if only my people would "practice" opening up to the gift. Yes, it is wrapped up with the misunderstandings of the ego, the ego which fears the voice because of worldly sin. The voice of the ego casts doubt on the

The Cleansing

Father's voice with the Holy Spirit. I promise you, if a soul practices listening to the Spirit, it will bring joy and comfort in this time and not have to wait for the next life. God's kingdom is truly within. Look at your life, Janine. How could anything have happened without the Holy Spirit and the ability for you to hear my voice? There would be no healing on this deep level. God's kingdom is meant to begin here on earth. Love as I love, child, with no judgments and a yearning to open and teach hearts the language of the Holy Spirit. Yes, there are sensitive times when you walk a tightrope with some souls because of the lack of trust in God. Also, some people you work with have closed hearts, but pray and be patient. I will help open the door or a window just like Pamela and, as you trust more in me, I will help.

Thank You, Mother, for my hands are truly blessed. Thank you for loving me and helping me to hear your voice and thank you for the cleansing. I truly feel my heart opening more and more to Ed's love. Guide me with the words as well as my spirit to love him as God intended.

December 10, 2012

Mother, what is it you wish me to write about?

Write about your bowels, child, what is it you feel?

I feel pain in my bowel area.

It is the pain you had to go through.

What do I do now, Mother, without Bethany and Sarah.

You will be with me and I will guide you. Yes, there is a loss and your tears reflect that loss, but I am with you always. You will feel the pain with me and through me from now on. You will feel my blessing and protection.

What do you feel now child?

My bowel is relaxed and no pain, Mother.

This is what I have come to show you, that the gist that comes to you through me is one of love and blessings. Now that the children have been freed, there is more room for us to do our work. There is the rage we need to exorcise, so be patient with

The Cleansing

these feelings for they shall be healed in God's time. For now, know that I am with you and the children are in God's care.

Bow your head and be with me.

Janine Lariviere — Coming Home to the Mother

Saying Goodbye to Sarah and Bethany

December 11, 2012

Mother and I went to the Garden together and she showed me Sarah sitting on Jesus' lap. She was naked with no fear. No fear. Just wonder at the beauty of Jesus. She was listening to him tell of the wonders of heaven. There was no need to worry about nakedness or abuse. Not anymore. Mother gave Bethany to an angel to be nurtured. My heart is sad and happy, happy for them, sad because I don't have that wonder. However, the Blessed Virgin has promised me I will in time. Sarah turned to me and waved. She had beautiful, long dark hair, beautiful dark brown eyes and a beautiful smile. Bethany was beautifully round and healthy with hazel eyes, a beautiful infant.

Right now my heart is broken. Mother, I need help to carry on. I denied them for so long and only have known them for a brief moment. Now they are gone.

Child, I am with you in your pain but I promise you, you will know them in the afterlife. They held all the abuse and now you are strong enough to take over. Now I can help you to release all the hurt, rage and sorrow that is within you. You will be set free because of my Father's love for you. Sarah and Bethany have done their work and are with the Father. I gave you a glimpse into heaven and be grateful to the Father for that. Remember this day and the day of the rapture for they will give you faith and a memory of God's love.

Saying Goodbye to Sarah and Bethany

December 12, 2012

Mother, what is it you wish me to write today?

Child, you have learned so much today.

Begin with the Grotto. Yes, your parents were involved as your aunt and uncle were. Janine, it was an elaborate sick system that spanned generations before you and sometime after you. It took place at the grotto as well as other places indoors. This is not just for your generation but for many generations to heal. Previous generations have asked the Father for forgiveness and they are with the Father but, as I have told you, the Father's house has many rooms and your ancestors are asking you to free them to a higher room. There is not the justice you know on earth that the Father seeks; it is to cleanse all souls. You are doing that now with your deep work and some souls do it in the hereafter. They pray for your courage as well and you will see your fruits when you see the Father and Jesus and myself. The angels and archangels dance in the light of your courage. It is not a sinful thing that you do when you hear my voice and bear witness to it. It is only fear and your ego that wants you to be so "loyal" to your ancestors. Loyalty has no place in God's kingdom, only the truth does. As I have taught you, it is the truth that sets all souls free. The saints in heaven are not all canonized, Janine. There are those who have learned of God's love by listening to his spirit, the Holy Spirit. For I tell you, child, in a loud and clear voice that the prophets have listened in the same way as you and they did not have the "noise" that you have had to filter out. They saw through the Holy Spirit just as you are doing now. Blessed are they who believe and do not see. You do not see with your eyes but with the grace of the Holy Spirit. You saw the beauty of Bethany and Sarah through my eyes and yet it is not the eyes of the human part of you. Be assured, child, you met Jesus as a small child only you didn't remember it. Just as the movie you saw when you were a child where Jesus came down from the cross to listen to a child in an attic, so Jesus came to you when you asked Him to. He came but not in the way you had anticipated. He sent me to watch and teach you. All those years of being so inside yourself gave you time to bear witness to the insanity, but also gave you time to be outside yourself to bear witness to the insanity (dissociation). It also allowed me to be with you and protect you and teach you the ways of my voice. It needed only time to bear the fruit you bear

Saying Goodbye to Sarah and Bethany

today.

As for the session with Don, I am pleased that you had the courage to say what I asked you to and asked Don to listen and witness what happened at the grotto. Yes, your mother is still alive and I hear you're wish to be loyal to her but, as I said, only the truth has a place in God's kingdom. The truth is the only path to the Kingdom. No, you are not lying; you are revealing the truth through me. There is no sin in telling my words. There are people who will believe and there are those who will not believe. This is not of your worry; the Father will work with that. You need only pray for the souls who have closed hearts.

Also, notice how your courage is contagious. Do not deny the courage that Don showed as well. How great is the Father's love and mercy! He chooses the time and the place. The angels and archangels worked as well to have you both experience that beautiful moment. Remember this day always, for it is the day that you both were given a blessed gift, the gift of a new beginning, a new and profound awareness of the love of God.

I heard your pain as you said goodbye to Sarah but Don is right, there is a new place for the both of you. She is outside of you and with the angels, but she is also with you as an angel.

Janine Lariviere   Coming Home to the Mother

A Birthing into the True Meaning of Love

December 14, 2012

Dream last night:

I am in a beautiful old country home, the home of my ancestors. I sit with a father and son and the son is very attentive to the old father. It is apparent that they have a beautiful relationship. There is a beautiful dark haired woman who comes into the room with a German shepherd dog on a leash. I kneel down and the dog licks my face and I am not afraid. I explain that I used to be terrified of these dogs and now I am not. I am a bit apprehensive but not afraid because I trust the woman. She would not put me in danger. She then takes the dog outside. I hear the son begin to clean up the father and prepare him for bed. I hear the rustling of clothes and look ahead so as to give them privacy. Then I hear the woman outside begin to exclaim, "Father Almighty, loving Father." She says it again and again and then people in the house as well as outside begin to say it with her. It begins to extend everywhere until the words become like a song praising God over and over again. It felt like it extended around the world.

Blessed Mother, give my hands the grace to understand this dream.

Child, hear me, for this is a dream from the Father.

The son is the Son of God who is in a loving connection with your father. The son is cleaning up the Santeria which is represented by your father. The woman is me cloaked in the wardrobe of a young woman bringing in the dog which represents your rebirth into your sexuality that was taken away so long ago (that rebirth you and Don experienced). You felt the love and hope from the dog, the love and hope of a birthing of your sexuality. The praises that I began outside of you have now expanded to inside of you and reaches out to the world. The praises you heard are those of those you have touched with your yes and now they praise God for the beauty of your wholeness. Every one of your ancestors will spend eternity singing those praises. Continue to praise Him as well and expand it to the outside world.

I prepared you for this prior to sleep. Remember your question to me about what to do in this moment and I said nothing, give it

A Birthing into the True Meaning of Love

to me and the peace you felt. This is what happens when you stop trying to do it all by yourself. Turn to me and breathe out the need to do. You need do nothing until I nudge you. I will not ask anything of you that brings doubt. That is just noise. The dog showed you that you need never be frightened, for I am there to stop any further damage to you.

Practice breathing out and letting go of the need to do. Breathe in and allow yourself to just be. I love you, child, go and share your love of God and me and it will extend outward. As the dream shows, it becomes contagious.

December 17, 2012

Mother, I am in pain but I come with the knowledge that you wish me to write.

There is no heaven or earth that will keep you from me. This is what you were taught, that I withdraw my love when you have been bad or worse evil. There is thievery going on here. Thieves have stolen your innocence and sense of self. The weekend was especially hard because of the isolation you feel. You do not fit anywhere just as in the dream last night. There is no one who knows you but Don and you became aware of it. People do not seem to hear you because of their own need to feel righteous. Because of what happened last Friday (The Blessed Virgin is referencing the horror in Newtown), *people have a need to find a place to put blame and there is none. There was an insane man who did horrible things and you need to pray for him and others like him because of faulty wiring. Child, you need not fear. You are not the author of these words and you fear judgment. I judge not*

A Birthing into the True Meaning of Love

and the Father judges not. I have given you a higher awareness even though it is very painful, for the world wants to judge this man and I want you to pray for him and his salvation and for the salvation of those sick people like your father who know no other way. He, like your father, went down a terrible path and felt no way out but to continue the insanity. Why do you feel such fear, child? I do not hold you responsible for these words nor do I fear who may see this writing. The world will know me by my fruits and I bring love and the hope of peace for all my children including this man.

Breathe, Janine, breathe in my love; let me take your pain away for I am the Mother of God and of the salvation of the world. He who comes to me will have the gift of the light of my womb. I am the Immaculate Conception and I bring the light of hope into the world. Please continue to give me your wounds. I like the way you wrap your pain, wounds and fears like a gift for me to take and heal. It is this and not just the glorious feelings that I want. I want the agonies of humans to be given up to the Father. The horrible feelings you have about yourself are the results of the shaping and not who you are at your very soul. Do you think I do not know that? God does not punish your imperfections. The world and others who think that are wrong. I come to heal the insanity. All humans have a deep sense of loss in their hearts; loss and woundedness. It is my love and the Father's love that brings order and sanity to a crazed world. Pray, please pray for all the lost souls.

Janine, I am with you here in this holy place and I am with you in the isolation within your family. I took your anger and cleansed it when you gifted it to me. Your anger and fear is understood, not by you yet, but by me and the Father.

Go now and love as I love. Love the worst of people, not just the best.

Yes, Mother.

Janine of the Sisterhood of Bernadette

A Birthing into the True Meaning of Love

December 18, 2012

What have you learned, child?

Oh my Mother, blessed Mother of God. I praise you and the heavens for all your grace. I have learned that by loving the worst in a soul, I love the way the Father loves. He wants nothing more than to heal sin and not punish it. The love of God knows no bounds. I have learned that your healing power is released when I give you my sins and am aware of it. You take it like a gift and heal it. The more I try to do it on my own, the more I feel the need to be perfect or I will bring down the wrath of God, the more I consume myself with angst. So I have learned that the power of your love works best when I turn my sins of thoughts or actions over to you.

Yes, child, you do well. Please use quotation marks around my writing from now on. They are my words and I ask you to have the courage to let the world know of my words. I promise you that I will bless you for this. I love all of God's children and remember when I told you that the day you see each of my children as the

most important person on earth is the day you know your value.

Yes, Mother, I remember.

Well, child, that day has arrived. You have done well with the souls you have sat with today. You have used the power of love by looking at and loving what you consider sin and blessing it and giving that to me and I am pleased with you. I am also pleased that you are using the quotation marks. It matters not what the world may or may not believe. The heavens are singing with the joy of your courage. There may be those who see this as blasphemy, but do not fear, the Father is pleased and his grace is upon you.

To the topic of sin, there are many more of those who have such hardened egos than those who do not know of God. They profess to have all the answers. Like the Pharisees they use the language of the church and self righteousness to try to prove the ego's point. Again, child, this is another example of shaping and or sin. Please, rather than judge it, love it for the ego is rendered helpless in the face of non-judgment and love. So, as you have begun to learn today, love the worst in a soul and that includes the fear of the ego. The ego fears annihilation and so it hardens to the language of love. So now, child, do you see? It is the same problem that Adam and Eve had. They allowed the ego to harden to God's love and it is the ego that needs the most love to

A Birthing into the True Meaning of Love

recapture its initial blessing.

Also, do you remember your covenant with Jesus?

Yes, Mother, I do. I was married into the spirit of God and as his bride I was given the covenant to do his will and his words will be my words.

Yes, child, that is correct and I do the same. Your words are my words especially in your healing ministry. It is time to begin to expand it and I will open the doors. You need only wait for my instruction. I will show you the way.

Be it done unto me according to your word. You bless me with your love. I do not do anything to deserve such love and grace. Mother, please know how grateful I am.

Yes, child, I know, I know your heart.

So, my loving child, you ask where we go from here? What about the children and the souls who do not know of me? We have discussed this before and they share a special place in God's plan for they do not have the biases of the church and all of its generational egos attached to it. They only know of the love or lack of love of their fathers and mothers and ancestors. It is to these children that God wants to extend his loving grace. Pray for those souls as they mature that they hear God's voice and do not suffer the church's managing of the topic of sin. Just as you learned to fear the devil rather than trust God's power over evil, my children of the church still suffer the feelings of hopelessness that they need to single-handedly overcome sin. So they try and try like you to make up for something that is impossible to do without God's loving presence. They need only turn it over to the Father and it is healed. The words Father, bless me for I have sinned are the only words necessary.

Let me say it again. A heart that is open to God's loving presence need only learn to do what you have done and that is to take the sin or shaping and wrap it up and give it to the Father or me or the Holy Spirit. As you have discovered, it becomes an impossible task when we try to use our ego to justify sin or we try to stop the sinning on our own. It cannot be done by the sheer power of the will. The will is another word that ego uses to trick you into trying to do it on your own. The will was meant to have the decision making power to choose God or not. Now over the generations it has become entangled with false choices because it is being driven by the powerful ego unless and until it is turned over to God. It becomes so entangled that it becomes the fodder for addictions, which by the way is another example of the ego taking over. Alcoholics Anonymous is an organization that knows this all too well. The only way to healing is to take the addiction and turn it over to the higher power of God to heal it. When a soul asks for help by realizing it cannot do it by a sheer act of will,

A Birthing into the True Meaning of Love

that is when the Father and the heavens are released to heal.

Thank you again, child, for writing my words and trusting that I will bring my words into meaning later. The world needs to know that you write only the words and as you write they make little sense until you go back when we are finished. Go now and love as I love.

December 20, 2012

Mother, what is it you wish me to write?

Child, I need you to write about the noise, the noise that comes from the wounded ego. It is diminished, as I have said before, with love and tenderness and by turning it over to me. You have just witnessed the panic leave you as you write. I wish the world to know how much courage it takes for you to write. Yet each time you begin, the fear and panic is relieved. Why do you think this is so? My child, when you put your hands on these keys despite your fear, you come to this holy place and despite your fear you ask me my wishes. I wish the world to know that it is the fear of your ego that causes your panic. Not all souls feel this to this degree but all souls feel the pull to not believe things they cannot see. Yet you can bear witness to the world of the graces that come upon you when you come to this holy place. So you ask how do I, the Mother, heal all this. I heal it, as you are learning,

A Birthing into the True Meaning of Love

by your giving it back to me. Pray that all souls learn this lesson. Turning the ego over to me is just like giving me a gift of love and I will heal all the anger, pain and sin. It is just like turning over a new leaf. Only I am the beginning and the end of all forgiveness, for I carry within me the light of the world. Just as you carry the light of the birthing of your children, so I gave life to the Son of Man and I have all the privileges of the Son of Man. How loving God is to have given a woman, a human being, the rapture of giving birth to the Son of Man. That alone has given me all the rights of the Father and the Son and the Holy Spirit. Jesus became man and I was the one who gave birth to the resurrection and the light. So how would it seem such an impossible task to ask? Not at all. The Father keeps it simple. Original sin has cast the ego into the world and I and the Father and the Son and the Holy Spirit renew and forgive and bring hope into the world. The ego is so yearning for what you have, Janine, and that is my love; but it needs the light of the Father to see and hear that. Original sin is that which makes us all human and it is that part of us, the ego, that yearns to be back with the Father. It is so distraught that it makes up these fictitious yearnings such as money, power, fame and sexual prowess that it has lost itself in them. With the Father's love there can be a true healing on this earth. So, I now bring it back to the beginning of this conversation. You are in need of healing your ego for it still fears annihilation because it fears it has no value on this earth. Love as I love, Janine, and the false strength of your ego will lessen and lessen. I have heard your prayer and the giving over of your ego. Now I begin to teach you true love for yourself. It is time. You have learned to love the worst in others, now love the worst in you. Your ego was taught to take control over you so that you would not die in the face of all the pain. In this way it is no different than any other soul, but you have taken it to an extreme because of the woundedness. You have been so split from all those parts of you that your ego felt the need to pretend it is perfect. In that vein your ego developed a judgmental system. It made you feel better about yourself. Now your ego is beginning to relax and that is why you feel so differently and there is no need to judge. It still leaves you alone and isolated because you feel few will understand your love for me and the Father. It is time to risk exposing your love for me. I will show you the way. Follow my lead, child.

Thank you, Mother, you know my heart. Thank you for your patience. Bless me for I am a sinner. I used to think this admission was a terrible thing because it would bring me into the fires of hell, but you have shown me differently. I give it to you and ask you to heal it in your own time. How great you are, my loving Mother. I will love my ego and I ask you to continue with your love for me. Thank

A Birthing into the True Meaning of Love

you for allowing me to see the beautiful child today. Was it Sarah, Mother?

No, child, it was your beautiful ego. I gave you that picture so you will see that she is not to be feared, she is to be loved. She has a disarming smile, doesn't she? That is for you, my child. Go and love as I love and by the way I sing the praises of God with you. Keep singing.

December 21, 2012

Mother, I am here to do your will. What is it you wish me to do?

Write about the mountain, child, the mountain that you have climbed in order to get here. At times it was a mountain of hopelessness and at other times a small incline to traverse. The Holy Father has been with you as I have and this day is blessed for you. Look up and tell me what do you see.

I see the Grotto, Mother.

What is there?

There is a sadness over me for I know not the whole story of the pain there, only the bits and pieces.

Hear my words, child, the Father has given you a blessing. You will soon see the light of his light and the love of his salvation for the cure you so hoped for has been given to you.

Mother, my hands feel frozen and my heart feels so confused. Are these really your words?

A Birthing into the True Meaning of Love

Yes, child, your confusion is the noise at the Grotto. The Father has called those voices to rest for now and the voices of those you have saved are singing. Hear their song. So again I ask you to look up and tell of what you see.

I see and feel the light of God shining down on me even in the rain today and I am driven to tears. I fear damnation at this moment, the damnation of all those poor souls who have no hearts here. They have been destroyed in the fires of hell. There is so much pain and torture here. It is almost unbearable. Help me, Mother, for there is so much sin here.

Child, rest for a moment. The fear and panic you feel is not from being wrong, it is from being right. I know you would rather have me tell you that you are crazy right now, but you are not. What you witnessed was the hearts being torn out of the animals and the blood spread over the Grotto, a worship of the devil. Please trust me, child, you did not make this up. The light of heaven is upon you and the souls who did this are being cleansed in the light of your courage. God has blessed this moment. What these souls did was defile God's love and his words. Again, I tell you, child, there is a healing here today for you and the souls who are being freed here. Go and wait upon the Lord for you have experienced a healing here as well. Fear not my words, Janine, for they shall come to fruition.

Janine Lariviere	Coming Home to the Mother

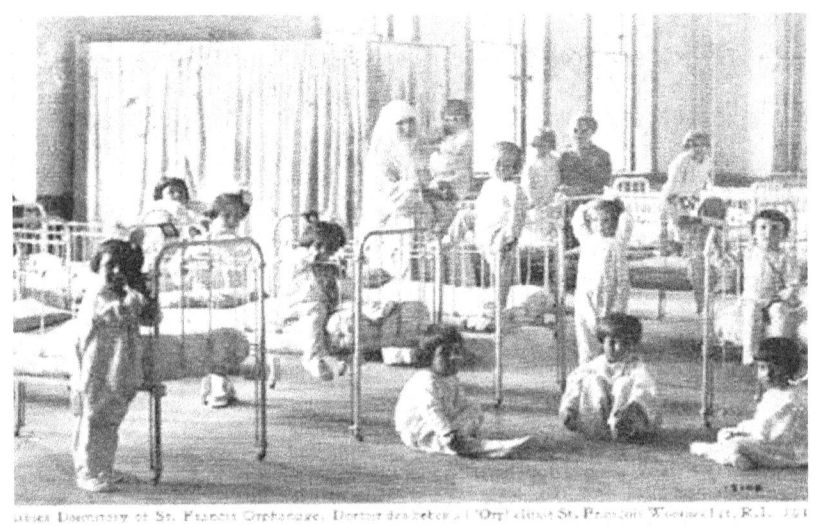

The Orphanage

A Birthing into the True Meaning of Love

December 26, 2012
Session with Don Today

Mother, please help me to tell the story just as it happened. Mother asked me to bear the pain of the sacrifices of the Santeria with her and I said yes. I felt the pain in my heart and she said her heart was bleeding too. She gave me a glimpse of her heart and it was so painful. She needed my body to express the intense pain of the defilement at the grotto. She made me aware of the need to express the pain for all the souls who were hurt there. She also wanted me to pray for all the souls who were driven to do such horrible things.

The Chapel in the Orphanage

Mother Speaks of Visionaries

December 29, 2012

Mother, what is it you wish me to write?

Child, this has become a blessed and sacred place. Be sure to have the Rosary with you in order to bless it with my presence. Go today with my blessing. There are many ways to reach my Lord and Father. This woman is blessed with a gift (Mother is referring to a medium that some of my husband's family had invited me to go to see). *She is not a witch so you need not fear for my Father is with you. Listen well and take notes and follow my heart. I will open your heart and voice. Trust in me. Those going will hear and pray that their hearts are open to the Father's words. It matters not how they open whether it be by a medium or a visionary such as yourself. Yes, child, I have given you such a title. Have you now discovered that I follow you everywhere? I am deep inside and I surround you as well. The light of the Father is with you as well. All of my children can find me if they choose me. It takes only a giving over and the heavens work to bring it about. Each has a gift embedded in their soul and can have it opened with prayer and a turning over to the Father.*

You are discovering my deep love for each of my children. As you noticed today, a warm loving smile is all that is needed. When you do not feel a door open or a nudge from me, all you have to do is smile with warmth in your heart and I will do the work with your prayers. Your prayers give energy to the process of opening the hearts of souls.

Thank you, Mother. You grace me with your loving presence. I wish only to be your loving child and love all of your children.

Mother Speaks of her Sick Children

December 31, 2012

Thank you for taking me into the Garden and praying with me today. Thank you for all your love in my time of confusion and misunderstandings. What is it you wish me to write?

Child, my dear child, notice how I address you for you are my child and so dear to me. I am Mother to all and judge not. I have the heart of a loving mother who cannot condemn. Your mother was so ill and so disturbed, child. Pray for her with me that God will bless her and keep her safe. She has such misguided ideas and she is so childlike that she absorbed it all just like you did but she was not sound enough to manage all the abuse. She has no malice but is often guided by the sins of those in her past. She did not have enough of a stable self to love her children as I love or as you love. She was underdeveloped. I know you forgive her but you still carry the wounds of her anger and hate. Yes, Janine, she tried to hurt you and even kill you by placing you in that box. It was not your aunt but your mother who put you in that box. I will answer your question about your father later but for now slow your mind down and just write. I am with you and your mother and all the generations that brought on this hurt and pain. It is not just for you that I am here. It is for all my children, those who are good and those whom people call evil. There are many rooms in my Father's house and there needs to be a different type of healing in each. Your mother's need for healing is entirely different than your father's needs. Yes, you heard from your grandmother through the medium on Saturday. As you witnessed, the medium has scenes that she witnesses. Some are noise and she is working on getting past the noise. Some are better at it than others and some are fictitious. What she saw was your grandmother who is with you as an archangel; that is why the medium said she is a very good woman. The medium saw her glow. She is part of your ancestors who pray with you to set those hurt children free. She was right about your father, mother, aunt and uncle. She is right about your aunt being dealt a difficult hand but so were all the others involved.

    To answer your question about your father, Janine; your father

Mother Speaks of her Sick Children

was blessed with forgiveness because he said yes to the Father but, as the medium said, he still needs to do some work. His hand gestures were of his addictions and he is ready to be freed from the chains that bound him. I ask you, child, are you willing to help in this matter?

Yes, my Mother, you know my heart and you know I am willing.

I ask because of free choice, my child. It needs to be a loud and clear yes each time I ask. I am grateful to you for your yes because it helps free so many of my children. Do you understand, child, your father and those of evil doing are all my children as well? Your yes will be difficult, but it brings so many home to their rightful place in God's house. The rooms, child, are those rooms as I have said that hold souls who have the same kind of healings needed. There are those who work for that healing here with me and those souls like you who work on your side. Do not take your work lightly for the ego wants to make light of it. When you are in the world for as long as you have over these holidays, it is easier to fall prey to the ego and feel that I have no place in your world. I have a different reality and that is why it is important to seek me out daily. That is why the Rosary brings me to you daily. It is not the secular world by itself that is bad, for many, many people have a hard time believing in me.

It is the fear that I may not be real that forces people to close their minds, because how could a loving God allow all this evil. He doesn't allow it per se. He gives all free choice and He cannot as an all loving Father take away free choice. I know your heart, Janine, and I answer your question as to why do some miracles happen and others not. It is by prayer and fasting and love that allows the heavens to move and work. Prayers after the horrible incident (the Blessed Virgin is again referencing Newtown) *are needed. Prayers for all those very sick people that are the lost souls of the world, lost in generational evil and sickness. Whether it is by evil or illness matters not, as much as prayer for all lost souls does.*

So, child, do you see how the Father keeps it so simple? It keeps coming back to prayer for lost souls and all souls that they may find the Father. I can't say it loud enough to you and the world. All that is needed is love, love of all my children. Because of original sin and shaping that love is so embedded in misunderstood beliefs that only prayer can bring about sanity to the world of lost souls. Just as you have such pain and angst in the times when you feel you have sinned that it pulls you away from me, all souls have that same fear and need to run rather than turn towards me and ask for help. Teach souls to turn towards me and all will be well. So the trip to the medium did not do any harm, it only taught you about the different rooms of my Father's house as

Mother Speaks of her Sick Children

well as some souls do have a gift of seeing images. They like you need to filter out the noise.

Go now, child, and pray with me for all lost souls.

January 2, 2013

Mother, what is it you wish me to write today?

Child, as you know, it was a painful day for you and, though you may have forgotten some of it because of the intense pain, I will remind you. Yes, there was so much pain at the grotto and that is what you saw and felt. Your arms are weak right now because of the intensity of the trauma that came out of your body. The Father is pleased with your courage as I am. Thank you for your yes again. Also, I know your heart and I am aware that you would die for me and I am pleased with the way you turn to me in the pain now. That is what pleases the Father. The pain that you allowed your body to witness was the pain of so many hurt by the Santeria. The screams that came from you were of the many who have suffered so much. Because of the witnessing to the truth, many shall live with the Father at the second chance. I will say it again. There are many angels and archangels who spring into

Mother Speaks of her Sick Children

action on the air of the energy of prayers and fasting and the Rosary. The energy gives rise to the air that allows the winged spirits to move heaven and earth to reach lost souls.

The pain you witnessed through your body gave rise to so much energy that the angels and archangels were able to take flight in a beautiful way so that others may know the Lord. The energy from one prayer gives flight and your prayer gave many, many flights into the heavens and earth. For that the Father is grateful. Thank Don for his ability to keep you grounded in the fact that there was no evil in you. Your fear was unfounded. He gave you back my words that there is no evil in you. He has heard my words and I am pleased with his efforts as well.

Now to the Santeria. Do not capitalize the name anymore for it is of the evil one and you cannot give it any power. The outside forces of the santeria are dangerous to souls and your witnessing today has put the energies into the universe to counteract such evil. I need you to write what was witnessed to. I know this is hard for you to hear again but I wish you to tell of the evils there. There were many children hurt, raped, and who died there. There was an underground baby making machine which produced babies that were never given a name or born in a hospital where there would be legitimacy. Yes, I make a very bold statement and your agony today was the witnessing of those that died there. I do not expect the world to believe me, but the Father needs you to witness to the defilement there.

You witnessed children and animals being hurt, raped and sacrificed to the devil. They made excuses that such defilement was a way to destroy the evil in the world. Can you understand such thinking? Of course not! It was a sick and deranged group of people who were of the devil. They had its parishioners believing that children who were sacrificed were going to be given up, so that the devils would be satisfied and leave their loved ones alone. There are generations of children who died there, Janine. What I showed you was not just your family but generations of defilement in that place.

You are not of the lie, they are. Be brave, my child, for your place with the angels and archangels is cemented. I will also bless the generations after to you as well for all your bravery.

Bless you, Mother, and thank you for allowing me to feel your love for me today. I now know the arms of a loving Mother.

Yes, child, that was a special blessing so that you may know the love of a mother's love. Go now and learn how to play. The Father wants you to know his love on this earth as well. It was meant to be enjoyed. Your path has taken a painful turn, but go now and see his blessings. Call your children and see their joys as well.

The Pain that "Growed-up Janine" has had to Feel

January 4, 2013

Mother, do you wish me to write today?

Yes, child. You are so full of fear, please accept my love and feel my love as I hold you close. The Father has blessed your pain for it is truly a deep, deep pain of all the wounds you carry. Stop and let the tears flow.

Now, child, write of the pain.

You know my heart, Mother. The pain is not the physical pain of being stabbed in my heart but the woundedness that brings out the tears and torment that feels like my heart is breaking. I have no one to hold me physically right now and I need your loving arms to bear this woundedness. Please be with me as I let my heart break. I cannot find any other words to describe this hurt and pain. It brings on so much isolation, so much aloneness, and so much torture to my heart. They could only do so much physical pain but the emotional torture keeps on and on and on.

Yes, child, I know your heart and the pain that surfaces like a strong wind that you cannot control. It is the heartbreak of both your woundedness and the woundedness of those tortured by the santeria. The Father and I are with you in your isolation. It is that same pain that led Jesus to the cross. He died for mankind so that they might not be tortured by the fires of hell. He died so that mankind can know the kingdom of Heaven.

But to get back to your pain, I am pleased that in spite of your fear you have come back to me. Keep turning to me. As you witnessed, I am with you in your isolation. When you cried out for me to be there and keep you from the insanity, I did. The insanity of having to be a witness to the insanity is the pain that you felt in your heart. Yes, it is difficult to describe but all of mankind knows of that isolation to a degree. You feel it for so many that it is compounded. As I said, the pain comes up like a wind and it takes you by surprise. When it comes up, find a place for you and me to sit. It will pour out and I will be with you. Yes, you needed to call Don to be reassured that you are not crazy.

Please follow me into the Garden and I will hold you there. Breathe in my love for it is a deep and powerful love that I have

The Pain that "Growed-up Janine" has had to Feel

for you. This pain has been coming out for so long and you are just now beginning to realize the depth of the pain that you are witnessing. You are just now allowing the flowing of the pain as it is necessary. You have turned to me and continue to turn to me. I hold you even when you can't feel me. So now how do you feel, my child?

I feel your tenderness around me and your love for me. I also feel the glory of being your child. Mother, you know my heart and how I had never known the hug or holding of a mother. Now you have allowed that to happen. Thank you so much.

Yes, my child, I have known your pain of never having been held by a mother and that is the blessing that the Father has poured into you. Do you not see the path now that the Father has laid out for you and the path that He has laid out for Don? He has been there while all this pain has been pouring out. Know that I am with you as well as the Father.

As for mankind, there is that hole of isolation that only the Father can fill.

As for the writing that I dictated a few days ago, it is a hard and painful story to absorb but it is a story the Father wants to be told. It is so difficult for you, Janine, but it is the truth of the grotto. That land has been fornicated and you are part of that pain and torture. The pain that wells up and comes out of you is an un-knowing pain that is nameless, yes, but it is pain and torture that you cannot fathom with your physical mind. It is a knowing in your body and that is what the Father feels as well. It is of such a magnitude that the Father experiences that pain when He sees his children cause such pain and destruction to other souls. Again, that is why the Father sent his Son so that it can all be forgiven.

The pain has left you weak, child, but I will fill you now and you will be light of heart again. In the very beginning, the Father gave you the map to all this healing and you have done well. Please teach your children and grandchildren to listen to the voice of the Spirit. I will show you the way.

Thank you, Mother, for all your blessings.

The Pain that "Growed-up Janine" has had to Feel

January 5, 2013

Mother, what do you wish me to write about?

My dearest Janine, let the tears flow. Bow your head and be with me. Stop and be with me for this time is for you and me alone.

January 8, 2013

My dearest Mother, what is it you wish me to write about?

Child, your devotion to me is wonderful and it does not go unnoticed. Your prayers and your saying of the Rosary many times a day is a loving matter and the Father is pleased at how you have turned to me.

Stop and listen, child. There is something of a drastic nature that the Father needs you to write about. It is of the santeria. What else can there be you ask? There is little time left for the time has come to witness to the truth. I tell you so that you can be wary for tomorrow's session. You will need the love and patience of Don and the angels, for you will be given much pain tomorrow. Fear not, the Father and I are with you. You shall see the pictures of those who have hurt you and it will be difficult to bear, but bear witness to it anyway. I know you fear that I am of the lie. But do not fear, for it will all come to pass, my child. You will see the glory of God come to pass as well. Call and ask Don for more

The Pain that "Growed-up Janine" has had to Feel

time.

This is not a matter of ego again, Janine, for the ego has nothing to do with this holy place. You have done as I have asked, even though you feel crazy and untrusting of my words at this time. The Father will bless it.

I called Don and he had no extra time.

Child, thank you for coming back. You ask that I give you something right now. Go outside and see what I have brought you.

There is nothing out there, Mother. What is it you wish to teach me? I have gone out three times now and there is still nothing out there.

Child, there is everything out there. There is the Father who is in the heavens.

I am so distraught, Mother. If you know my heart, then take away this anger or at least let me know you are here. There is nothing outside and there is nothing left in my heart. There can be no truth to all this, for my heart has turned to stone. I have nothing left and there is no room for me. You gave me a place and now you take it away. I have nothing left. If there is truly a heaven, there can be no place in it for me. I am nothing and I hate what you have done. You have tossed me aside and there is nothing outside. So, does that mean all this is a lie and there is no santeria?

Just the opposite, my child, this is the santeria. This is the evil that wants you to feel there is no hope. Don is right. It is time to go outside the noise. The noise that says it is not true and you have no worth. What a surprise that Don has a cancellation, so you have extra time tomorrow. Do I not work in strange ways? Did he not call in just the right time to show you what going outside means?

Yes, Mother, thank you. At first there was no extra time. Now there is the cancellation and we have the extra time. Forgive my lack of trust.

It is all forgiven, my lovely child. Trust is a process and each time you look at the small but timely miracles, you see me and the Father. That is what the Spirit is all about. Do not fear for your children, for what you will teach them is not a lie, it is of God and the Father.

The Pain that "Growed-up Janine" has had to Feel

January 9, 2013

Mother, do you wish me to tell of our session today?

Yes, child. The promise that I made to you yesterday has now come to pass. I showed you the santeria.

Tell what you experienced and Don witnessed to.

Yes, Mother, your will be done in all things. Help me to remember all of it and exactly as it happened.

I brought in the picture I drew of you and the writing from last Wednesday and read it to Don. As I got to the part about the "baby making machine," I felt like Don would not believe it and that I was going insane. Don not only believed it, but he had heard of such horrible cults. I heard your voice tell me to look at the man of the santeria and it was my father. My father was part of the cult and he was part of the dismembering of the animals. I saw animals dying in agony and blood and I saw the understanding that he is not my father. He gave me up to other men as well and I was covered in animal blood. I was raped by my father and other men in a ritual that gave me to the devil. They raised the sexual experience into a worship of the devil in order to make it look legitimate. Because I was not his, it made it all "right." So in that way he and my mother and the others blamed me for being illegitimate. I also saw the entire picture of what all the alter personalities held. A crucifix being put into my vagina and the men each are taking a turn to rape me. I also saw the young men who were being brought into it like an initiation into the cult. I was aware in an instant what each alter had held and all the truth of the paths each alter took to get me to this day. At one point I was so sure that I was of the devil that Don asked if he should get the holy water and you said no, that you were protecting me. Otherwise, there would have been a need for an exorcism. You said we will need the holy water when we go to the grotto. Don also said that he felt that the statue of you was no mistake, that it was erected to try to bless the land. I felt the same way. The actual abuse took place closer to the small statue of a saint that faces my aunt's house.   I became aware in an instant that you said the book was to be called "Coming Home to the Mother." In that instant I knew why you saved me and that as horrible as the pain of those scenes were, that all would be well with me. I told Don the name of the book and asked him to remember it as well because it will be important in the future.

The Pain that "Growed-up Janine" has had to Feel

Did I forget anything, Mother?

Only that you are now whole. Yes, all those scenes were parts of the whole story that the alters held as well as Bethany and Sarah. The fetuses of Jane and Rachel were in that picture. There were too many men involved for you to know who fathered them. As for the young men involved, they were victims also. The animals were tortured as well and that was what you saw. Yes, they covered you in some of the blood and that is the blood you saw. I tell you this, not so souls will feel sick, but to have you and Don witness to the truth. I also tell you this so that souls will understand the need for the Father to expose such degradations. The Father's will is to save all souls, Janine, and many have asked for forgiveness. Those souls are involved in your healing as well as other tortured souls of such horrific abuse. Bless you, my child, and ask Don to write of what he witnessed as well. Go and rest. When you come back there will be more insights into the world of the Father.

A Blessed Keepsake of Our Lady of Lourdes

The Pain that "Growed-up Janine" has had to Feel

Don's Experience

"I experienced Janine agitated and struggling not to have to believe what Mary revealed to her about the horrible violence done to animals and children and who were the persons doing this. Then I was present to Janine releasing through her body not only her pain but also the pain of many children. I was blessed to be able to remain trusting and able to later share with Janine what she indicated she might not remember. During the intense and prolonged release, I found myself praying, knowing that I was meant to be the physical presence, reassuring Janine that what she was saying yes to was being true to Mother and deepening her own trust that what was coming out was true. Each time I read what Mother has asked Janine to write, my trust in this revelation and mission given Janine deepens. It was beautiful to experience Mother's quick "miracle" to give Janine the extra time she might need. As often happens, I experienced a time of quiet and peace after the releasing and sharing. No words needed, just peace, a healing and quieting peace. I again am confounded and in awe that God and the Mother of God bless me with a part in her message meant for so many through Janine."

The Pain that "Growed-up Janine" has had to Feel

Later in the Day

Mother, do you wish me to write? I am here with gratefulness and gratitude because I feel your loving presence. I thank you for helping me get through this day with energy to spare. I was so sick after the session and you have given me strength.

Yes, child, I have blessed you with strength. You need not worry about what has come out anymore. I have blessed you with wholeness now and the Father will take care of the rest. Will there be more pain you ask? Yes, but now you have the story and the rest is just icing on the cake of truth. I lived and walked the earth just as you, my child, and there were days of doubt in me as well. I trusted as you trust and I had to watch my Son die. The pain was unbearable but necessary. Just as for you, child, the pain was unbearable but necessary. You had to get those words of anger out yesterday and you gave it to me in all your anger. That gave me permission to heal it. It is not just in the good that we turn to the light. It is also in the anger that is often uncontrollable that we need to give it to the light. Even the confusion, anger and hurt at the thought that I had abandoned you needed to be given over to me so I could bring it to the light for you.

It is not of will power that saves us, it is the giving over of our will so that the light of God can heal. As I have said before, the minds of souls think that with research and databases they can solve all of the woes of the world by themselves. I tell you, child, that you cannot. The complicating factors are too much for the race of humans to do on their own. When you take the light of God out of the mix, you bring chaos and eventual doom to your efforts. On the other side is an easy fix. That fix is to bring a request to me or the Father or the Son to join in the efforts and watch all the chaos disappear.

Did not your confusion disappear today when you called for me? I brought the light of truth to you. The clear understanding of what happened had no confusion as well as the clear understanding of the book I will write and the name that you need to call the book.

There is no coincidence here. I gave you clear insight into the events of the santeria and am now giving you clear insights into the way of the salvation of the world. When you turn to me even in your anger and rage as you did and even with your hatred of me, you were still able to wrap it up and give it to me instead of

The Pain that "Growed-up Janine" has had to Feel

turning away (even though you and I both know you wanted to). I was able to take it, and not just heal it but make it a prayer for all lost souls. Just as I taught you to love the worst in souls, I have now showed you how I can love the worst in you with no condemnation.

Do you see now, my child, how the Father works? Instead of chastising your children all you need do it to teach them to turn to me. They have an inborn, innate awareness of the Father's love. Rather than chastise children (this is different from guidance), you need to teach love and turning to the light and turning it over. When people have lost the will to live, it is because they have no hope of redemption. The hope is in the light of salvation. Chastising and punishment only teaches hopelessness, the greater the chastising the greater the walling off of the heart. Can you see child, what I am saying. The Father teaches.

Follow the Father's ways and see the children prosper. Love and turning to the Father brings an open heart. Guilt has its own pain. Guilt is a way of realizing we have sinned but oftentimes we use it to control our children rather than guide. When a child does wrong, you were taught that teaching means punishment. I say use the power of the light to teach. Jesus taught in parables and stories and that is the way to teach your children. Teach by using stories. If a child steals, tell of a story about how stealing hurts another soul. Do not punish and forbid them to do anything. That teaches a child to feel humiliation which closes a heart.

So, child, it is late. Enough for today but ponder what I have told you. When you come back, I will have more insights for you to share with the world. Yes, the world will know my truths through you and the world will know that you alone are not capable of such insights. This is what happens when you turn to me and the light. I bring you to the light and I bargain for you with the light. Go now and place the name of our book at the top of your writings. Ask Don to help with laying the foundation of the book.

Mother Speaks of the Taliban

January 10, 2013

Good morning, Mother. Do you wish me to write?

Yes, my child. I wish you to write about the Taliban today. They are a classic example of anger, rage and shaping. The Father wishes you to tell of the hurt his heart has over such lost souls. Like the santeria they have a sick view of the way the Father's world works. They are especially difficult to help to see the Father's loving ways. Pray for them and in time you will build a prayer group to help in that effort. Watch for the doors that I will open for you. They are my children too, Janine, and I hurt that they may not see the light of God's love in the second chance. That kind of following is so closed and cold hearted. Only prayer will send the angels and archangels to stave off their possible inability to say yes to the Father at the second chance.

I know your heart and I know your trepidation, but I tell you loud and clear that all hearts in heaven break when a child of God says no to Him. As I have said before, all are born with the heart of God and one lost child leaves an empty space. Please pray especially for those in the Taliban and other hateful organizations like the santeria that God may open their hearts to see his love. These people have taken anger and hate and used it to justify hurting and killing people and even killing themselves. Yes, you may have killed their representor, but you have not opened his followers' hearts. So the destruction will continue.

Do you see now, child, that again only with prayer and fasting and the Rosary can we hope to stop this from happening. In the right place and time, the Father can send his angels and archangels to open hearts, but He needs the power of prayer in his healthier children to help heal his sick children. So, do you see that your yes is a yes to all nations as well? Your yes has brought you so many blessings as well. The Father wants only what is best for his children. As a loving counselor you have witnessed to what a loving mother does when one child is sick. That mother works so hard to help that child and make sure the world does not abuse that sick child. Likewise you and the healthier ones in God's world need to work and pray for God's blessings on his sicker children. Have I made it clear to you, Janine? Ponder my words today and come back with your questions. For now you are aware that my blessings are upon you. I will answer your questions for all the world to see and understand the Father's love for his children. Ask Don to come with his questions as well. Also, ask him to work on your grammar.

Our Lady of Fatima

The Inner Road to the Holy Spirit

January 10, 2013

Mother, I am back today, Do you wish me to write?

Do you have any questions, my child?

Mother, you know my love for you. How do I gain the courage to spread my knowledge of you? I am so fearful.

I know, my child. Patience and let me open the doors. As you have witnessed, it becomes a work of love, and peacefulness comes when it is time. Yes, I ask and sometimes you feel fear but you listen to my request and peace comes. This week was the exception, for what you heard from me was so hard for you to process. Hearing of the baby making machine threw you into a place of fear that you would be perceived as making it up. That sent you into a traumatic response, the same traumatic response as when you were a child. You became terrified and numb and then the rage hit. Once again you were being abandoned and called crazy for it was those few times that you reached out that you were made to feel crazy. I am always with you and I move you in loving ways and, as you have seen, it is in the nudging that I work my miracles. These last few days forced you to trust me in a new way.

Think to years ago, to the voice that asked you to kneel on the road and give the Father your will. You did and all the while not sure if you were crazy. I shall now explain, my child. I was there and watched as you were being prepared by the Father. You listened but you felt so embarrassed and humiliated. That is as bad as it will get from now on. I promise you that there will be those who will be very skeptical, but there will be more who will believe me through you. Fear not, my child, I am and always will be with you. I shall be there when others try to negate my writings. Let them know it is me they negate and that is all you need do.

All the Father wants is to begin to put this generation in touch with the inner wisdom of the Holy Spirit. It is the Holy Spirit that rises within us. It is a beautiful entity that can rise in each of us if we only begin to listen. It takes time and patience. Now this is a place that may begin with meditation but is not necessary.

The Inner Road to the Holy Spirit

Meditation teaches us to listen, but it is not the only way. As you have done, so can all other souls. Begin by asking for help filtering out the noise and listening to the Spirit that never, never chastises. The Spirit only moves in the most loving of ways. Then as you did, my child, you never, never judge any opposing voices. You merely ask for the grace to filter out what is noise and what is not. Those of the santeria did not learn to filter out the noise and so it left room for the evil one to use the ego to become grandiose. This invites sin and evil to come in. It is always, always necessary to bring the Holy Spirit and the Father or myself into the practice of learning the Spirit's voice. It takes the Holy Spirit to filter out the noise. As you learned, that noise can be very loud and frightening in accordance with the amount of painful shaping souls have experienced.

So now, my child, you are ready to begin to teach on how to hear the Spirit. I will open the doors, so you need not fear. You will hear me loud and clear just as you have in the last few days. I am aware of your fear. It is merely a fear of making a mistake and I tell you loud and clear that there are no mistakes. There is still a small lingering of noise but that too will soon disappear. Yes, you have my word.

Thank you, Mother, you know my heart and I love you so much. You have saved me from so much sin and I am truly grateful because now I know why I was allowed to live. I am grateful that you spared me so that I may be an instrument for you.

Yes, child, I know your excitement to do my work. This book is being written by me. But know this: I have been given the word from my Father that this is right and his timing is perfect.

January 12, 2013

Mother, do you wish me to write?

Yes, child, write of the Father's love for his children. Now you know the difference between the noise and my voice. The Father has such love that He not only gave man his Son, but also gave the Holy Spirit, so that man might know Him in this life on earth. What you now give witness to is that even the most closed and hard of hearts can find the Spirit of God.

Yes, child, the santeria closed your heart and the prayers of others sent the Father to move the heavens to bring salvation to you and many. You were but an infant when your heart was forced to close. How horrible and unfair, I know. That is what happens to many of God's children. That is why the Father instilled all souls with his heart.

So that beneath all of the pain and cold heartedness his love is always there. The Father knew your path as He mapped it out even before you were born. As I have said before, He places a soul in just the right family and in just the right circumstance to help bring his love and healing into that family. Because of choice, however, it is not always possible to do in a swift and linear fashion.

So you ask, does a soul choose a path before birth. No, not in the way you perceive. The Father works through his Son and the Holy Spirit to bring about his intentions. He loves into life a child to give hope to the generations. Yes, it is a mystery and one that you will understand when you are with me, but for now know that the power of prayer opens all doors for the Father to do his work. It counteracts all evil. In that way the prayers work like an arrow to spear evil. Remember the story of St. Paul and how the Father reached him. It was the power of prayer that allowed the angel to knock him off his horse. Likewise it is the power of prayers that send the arrow or bullet of healing.

I use the words of bullet or arrow to show you how fast and decisively the Father works. The arrows and bullets are his angels and archangels that go out to kill evil. He does not kill his children, only the evil. So now, child, are you beginning to understand the answer to your question about choice? Let me go further. When the Father sends arrows (the angels and archangels) to slay evil, there is room in a heart to see Him. Then a clear choice to choose

The Inner Road to the Holy Spirit

Him can be made. The sooner He slays evil, the sooner his children will be of clear hearts and the more likely they are to choose Him. In that way there is truly free choice. Those of closed hearts by and large are in the throes of evil or what you call shaping. The Father knows this, child, but he cannot interfere (another mystery that will be revealed) until prayers allow him to use his arrows to defeat evil. Child, I know your heart. It is a bit clearer but, because of your humanness, parts are still a mystery.

Mother, may I praise you. I love being with you and my heart is at such peace with you. It is, as you know, so hard to leave you to go back to the other world. Help me with this.

Yes, child. Write as I dictate so that all souls may know of my love. What you have been doing these last few days is what my desire is for you. It will become clearer and clearer as you sit with souls. I see you search for me and invite me to sit. You also ask what I look like and tell of my response.

Mother, you sit in the empty chair and take on the appearance of the patient. You teach me to look at each soul as you do.

Yes, child, now let me teach you why. As you have noticed, I point out your prejudices so that I may cleanse you of them. As you invite me to be with you (remember the need to say yes so that it becomes a prayer), I have the power to do the Father's will and that is to cleanse you of your prejudices. This is not the place to name them but you and I know of your sinful prejudices. Each time I join you in that way, I show you your shaping and am able to cleanse you a bit more. As you do this, there will be less space between the two worlds and less and less feelings of being in two separate worlds.

Also, child, notice how open you are to allowing your sins to surface in a nonjudgmental way. That is how the Father works. There is no judgment, just a loving cleansing. As you have noticed, the sins fall away at this kind of cleansing. Trying to loosen your own prejudices by a sheer act of will does not work. Be patient, my child, for the Father will reveal his ways more and more to you and with prayer He will send his arrows to slay evil. Continue to pray and as always I pray with you. Also, my child, just write. The punctuation and grammar can be done later.

Yes, Mother. Thank you for allowing me to be your fingers today.

You are welcome, child.

Later in the Day

I am pleased that you have made such a beautiful space for me so that I can tell the world through you of the Father's love. Yes, my child, I shall tell of the love of the Holy Spirit. The Holy Spirit comes in a whisper to all who ask for help. At first, as you learned, the whisper gets all mixed up with the noise of the ego. Then with a quiet heart, the Spirit's voice becomes clearer but never gets loud or burdensome. The voice of the Spirit waits for an invitation or a questioning. As time passes and one sits and invites the Spirit, the Spirit becomes clearer. It may be different for each soul but the process is the same. When you were a child, because of the need for you to split your experiences off, the voice of the Spirit was walled off as well. As you worked toward integration, you learned to differentiate between the noise and the Spirit.

The real work began over the summer months when you asked for help with the insanity you felt while taking the opiate based medication which triggered your memories and made you feel insane. Your prayers set the Spirit in motion and in that state you began to hear my voice. The Father prepared you for this in your infancy, Janine, and it has all come to pass through your surgery. So, do you see how some events help to set up the Father's will? You have been able to hear me precisely because of this. How great is the Father to have saved you and brought me to you from the very beginning. Tell of your experience of me (for others it will be the Holy Spirit).

Oh, my loving Mother; I am so blessed. I am aware that I have done nothing to deserve this. This is a gift and I am so grateful. I see the wonder of your teachings. I am using your words already to help others, as you know. To be able to tell a patient to tell a story rather than punish has brought hope and peace into a few people already. It makes so much sense. I wonder why we need to punish.

Yes, my beautiful child, there is no need to punish. The Father does not punish. He loves the way I and the Holy Spirit love. I feel your freedom to be and to not feel so unloved as you did. There is so much hope when we turn to the Father. It brings freedom. That freedom allows you to just be and to not use the outside world as a ruler to measure yourself by.

There needs to be a turning around of the way souls see the Father. If this generation can feel his love, the next will lose all fear. Yes, I make a bold statement in the Father's name. There is too much punishment which brings the need for a soul to wall off in childhood and then the ego has to take hold in a dangerous way. That was not the initial role of the ego. More on that at a later time; for now it is enough to know that you need to teach the way the Father does, with total love and the giving up of fear of punishment.

Later in the Evening

Child, how did it feel this evening to not have experienced that prejudice?

My Mother, thank you so much. You have shown me so much about the power of prayer. I have tried for so long to use willpower to stop thinking that way and, only when I stopped hating that part of myself and turned it over to you, it healed. It is gone and I can love this person the way that you love. Not only that, Mother, you helped me to have the courage to speak on that difficult topic of misunderstood loyalty. For that I am truly grateful. You have taught me to love myself, sins and all. Please, Mother, continue to show me my sins so that I may turn them over to you?

Yes, my child, I shall.

Mother Tells of the Father's Garden

January 14, 2013

Mother, thank you for taking the ache in my heart away and taking me into the Garden. What is it you wish me to write about?

Child, I wish to tell of my Father's Garden today. Do not fear. Your writings come from me and you are doing well. The ache is the fear of making a mistake. I tell you loud and clear - you are writing my words and wishes. The Father has such a beautiful place waiting not just for you, but for all his children. He brings such hope as you know. There can be no hope in everlasting life without Him, so my wish is for you to write as I dictate. The Father's house has so many beautiful rooms. They take your breath away. Heaven is not a static place. It is a beautiful place that has colors beyond your imagination. The beautiful rainbow I showed you is but one of them. Also, look at your heart right now. Is it not a heart of openness when just a few minutes ago you were filled with the fear that I am but a part of your imagination? How silly you are, child. I am here and do I not let you know each time you turn to me?

Yes, Mother, but sometimes it takes me awhile to think of turning to you because of fear.

Yes, child, I know your fear and I have taken it away again just as I always do. Come and let me show you the Garden of the Father. In one room are the children that are being nurtured by the angels and archangels, so that they may know the ways of the Father. Do you see your children there?

Yes, Mother, I see Jane and Rachel. I am sad that I don't know them yet.

Do not be sad for they are in my Father's house. They have the love of the Father and the angels and archangels. See the beauty of the flowers in my Father's Garden as well as the different animals that the children play with. The animals here have no need to kill for they are as tame as the fallen snow. The children will learn my Father's ways of total love through this Garden of play. Do not fear, my child. It is my wish that the world know of my Father's Garden through you. It is time. Souls have thought of heaven in such a nocuous way that the Father's beauty and love

Mother Tells of the Father's Garden

have been hidden.

Rather than excitement, the past generations and this one as well (although my Father is changing all of that) have learned to fear heaven. Statements like, "If God is alive and real why does He let such horrible things happen," gives the world the wrong idea of a loving God. Rather, the Father loves so much that he gives us choice, and as I have said before, some of those choices are made because of original sin and shaping. It is my hope and prayer, Janine, that the world will see the love of the Father in this life as well as in the next. If all souls looked at the love of the Father and turned to Him even with their doubts and anger, He would be able to take away all sin. It is not the sin but the turning to God that matters.

To get back to the Garden, my child, I wish to tell of a very special room, one that the Father wishes me to tell about. It is the room of your ancestors. How easy it is to forget your ancestors. However, in this room they pray for you and yours and work as the angels and archangels to send the Father's arrows to kill sin and open the hearts of his children. In this room there is such joy at aiding the Father to reach souls. It is a glorious place that holds those followers of Jesus. There is no need to be punished here, it is all about love. There is no need to make up for sins here. It is all love. The greatest of sinners are able to be with the Father and to work with the Father in heaven.

The word work is not the word as you know it. It is a word that tells of the Father's total love. He loves so much that He shares Himself with all those that say yes. He loves so much that all have equal place with him. There is no need for jealousy here, Janine. The Father's house may have different rooms according to the work to heal those who need to be healed, but in no way is it punishment. The healing is a healing just as you experienced that night of the four hours of burning. That night when you were healed in my company was a rapture that knows no bounds. That is why I told you to never forget these two raptures that the Father has given you. They are but a small picture of the Father's Garden. Now do you know of the Father's Garden?

Yes, Mother.

Now, child, the Father and I will guide you to the next phase of your journey. He wishes it to continue to be written. At the right time it will be given to the world in a way that will let his children know that his coming is to be looked forward to and not feared. His coming will bring the heavens here to his people. His coming will bring back the body. There is still work to be done because the Father has yet to be able to reach his children in such a way as to have the world see Him as a benefactor and not a source of punishment.

Mother Tells of the Father's Garden

January 16, 2013

Mother, please be with me. Do you wish me to write?

Yes, child, I am with you and yes please write as I dictate. As I look upon what you have done today, I am pleased as is the Father for you allowed me to give you the pictures to aid in telling the rest of the story of the santeria. The pictures brought on so much pain and the Father is pleased that you had the courage to allow Don to be a witness to it. The Father can now do his work to free those of the santeria. As I hope you can now see, there was an exorcism of sorts. Let me explain what exorcism is in the Father's world. There is a need to let out the pain and suffering of a sinful past so that the Father might end sin. It is a form of bloodletting so that the sins may be forgiven. When a soul is in the throes of such a sinful and evil doing such as the one you experienced, there is a need to have an intercession with prayer to exorcise the evil. The Father brought me in so that there was only the need for you to bear witness to the evil.

Some souls are so engineered by evil that it is absorbed into their body and spirit and gains a strong hold. For example, what you went through today was what you absorbed at such a young age that you have carried it into adulthood. Today the hold was loosened and freed. Child, I know your heart and yes, you were held by the evil of the santeria. They made it appear to be such a beautiful event that you were made to feel like a special princess. They brought the evil to a spiritual place albeit mixed with the sexual experience. That is why the Father is so appalled. They took his name and used it to do their dirty deeds and that is why you have carried this mixture of humiliation and sexual feeling. Do not fear, child, there was no sin on you. I did not allow it. There was, however, a need to free you from the throes of evil. The Father works to do this for all those in the throes of evil. He works and waits and hopes for others to say "yes" to Him so that He may put the forces necessary into place to free all his children. Praying and saying the Rosary and fasting for those souls in such throes aid the Father as well.

The Energy of Prayer and Fasting

January 16, 2013

Now, child, I know your heart and I will answer the question of "fasting." Fasting is not only a staying away from food so that it becomes a prayer. Fasting is stopping, listening and just being with oneself so that the Holy Spirit may enter a soul. Even in the quietness, souls continue to run from me and the Father. The operative word today is "bored." So many children are taught that boredom is a bad thing. How silly. Do you ever get bored anymore?

No, Mother, never because I turn to you and you are such a beautiful and loving company.

Yes, child, that is a gift of the Spirit. So to get back to the fasting, all of the addictions are ways to run from the Lord as well. Fasting is merely the becoming still and finding a place to invite the Spirit in. When I talk of prayer and fasting, I mean the Rosary which is a structured prayer, but I also mean fasting to be a form of prayer. When you sit and invite me in, it is a form of fasting. It becomes a prayer for the many. It allows the Spirit to open a soul's heart and the energy ignited becomes a prayer. Souls may also ask for God and the Spirit to help them and that too is a form of prayer, but your generation fears that form of prayer as well. They say "How can I ask God for anything when I don't go to church or say thanks to Him."

I tell you, child, loud and clear that the Father does not differentiate between the forms of prayer. He wants all of his children to come to Him. If a soul does not get his prayer answered in real time, however, does it mean He does not exist? Not at all, it merely means He cannot fulfill your request either because the timing is not right or it will cause harm.

As you know as a mother, it is not always possible to fulfill all requests. Again I speak of prayer and the prayers of fasting. In order to learn the ways of the Father, one needs to turn away from addiction and be still enough to hear the Spirit. As those who have addictions and attend AA are well aware that there is a need to turn to God first and then allow Him to do his work. It is the turning over, as I have spoken of before, that allows the Father to heal his children.

My will is that souls understand the role of prayer and fasting and the Rosary. These forms of prayer allow the Father to work his miracles and heal his children.

So, my child, let me say it again. The ability to fast means a slowing down and turning to the Father. Food is such a large part of our lives that giving up a food forces us to stop each time we are faced with that food and forces us to think of why we are giving it up. In that way it is a turning to God. I say this to you, that any way of turning to God the Father is a form of fasting. It forces us to stop and listen and turn to God. That being said again, stopping oftentimes is not stopping. It merely gives the quietness over to another form of busyness.

As you learned at such a young age, it was the busyness of the mind that kept you at a distance from yourself and thus from God. Getting in touch with yourself forces you to get in touch with the Spirit deep within you and forces you to see the loving Spirit within you. So now, child, do you see how my loving Father and I work? With patience and the prayers of your generations I have had the energy and power to move mountains. So that after all these years of your self-absorption, I have been able to help you to sit still and process all the pain and open up the spirit deep within you. Hence, your ability to hear me.

Go and pass on the good news that the Father is here at hand for all those who wish to find Him. Also, let the world know that any soul who can bear witness to another's story acts on my behalf and that it opens a heart. That is what I have been teaching you these last few months. Go and teach others.

Also, yes, let Don know that it is time to begin to allow a "testing of the waters." He has chosen well.

"Coming Home to the Mother" Detailed

January 17, 2013

Mother, do you wish to be with me?

Yes, my child. I am pleased that you have come to me and wish to spend time in my company. The Father has given you many blessings. I know your heart and there is a gratitude exuding from you now. There is the love of my Father that you now carry. I taught you about what coming home to the Mother means today. Let me explain because you have forgotten. I took you home today. Home to the truth of what truly happened on that hill. It is enough that the world knows that the pictures I showed you were of the foundation of the santeria. What I showed you was not only coming home to the truth but also coming home to me. It was I who gave all the alters each part of the whole story and it was I who took you in that very first moment of the horrific abuse. I, yes I, came to protect you. This very day, today, I brought you back there so as to take you home. Hence coming home to the Mother. That is why you are to name the book The Coming Home to the Mother.

Not only that, Janine, I have now given you the way to conceive of a way to bring all the nations into a global prayer group..... In the Father's time it will come to fruition. You call it e-commerce, I call it e-prayer. I will help you and introduce you to the people who will help in that endeavor. Your imagination is of the Father as well, my beautiful child, and yes His vision is to have souls all over the globe commit to prayer. There shall be a global chapel on line where souls will meet and share their prayers. So on any given day and on any given moment someone all over the globe will be praying the Rosary. It will be in God's time, child. So be patient and He will open the doors. I am pleased about the website, but be patient for I will send the right people to aid you when the Father deems it to be the right time. It is late, child. Go and rest and come back tomorrow for I have more blessings for you.

Thank you, Mother. I love you and please continue to allow me to be in your holy company as well as help me to be in the company of Bernadette. I know she loves you and was your voice so long ago and now you have blessed me to be your voice today.

Yes, child, the Father has chosen you in the same way as Bernadette.

January 17, 2013
Later in the Day

Mother, thank you for blessing me with your company.

You are welcome, my child. I am aware of your love for me. I am also aware of how you come to me now and relish our time together. There are outside world obligations, I know, and that is hard for you. However, know that I am with you always and you will hear me always. Your counseling practice goes well and you are hearing my voice guide you more and more. Yes, child, I know what you have learned in school and previously thought was the "gold standard" in counseling, but I have come to show you a different way. You do not need fancy words and behavioral techniques (although they can be helpful) to truly help souls. Just as you witnessed to today, when you sit and aid souls to just sit with their deeper self, it stops the noise and the truth of the deeper self comes out. The painful truth that lies in their hearts comes out.

You often fear sitting with souls because you feel inadequate to help them. Yes, you are inadequate by yourself. When you slow the process down and allow me to enter, I am allowed to do my work unobstructed. Your profession has learned to feel the need to always have the right answers but I tell you, child, only with the help of the Holy Spirit and myself will souls heal. Yes, you went to school and have a basic understanding of the "rules." But I tell you loud and clear that that is not enough. You need my help and or the help of the Holy Spirit to truly aid a soul to find itself in the quagmire of today's insanity. Do not fear your confusion. It is good. I have brought in confusion precisely because you need to let go of some of your clinical teachings. You also need to let go of your fear of making a mistake. That fear is imbedded in your need and the need of your profession to know all the answers.

Your confusion allows me in, my child. When you feel the confusion, I hear you turn it over to me and I can move in and help open a soul. Stop and listen for I am here with you. There is no more need to run. Stop your running and listen to me. I come in the quietness of a private moment and I come in the quietness of a counseling session. Notice how beautiful this morning worked when you said nothing and allowed that beautiful couple to ponder and reach deep within themselves. I also nudged you to stop the noise when they went to the noise. They respected your doing this because they need help in stopping the noise. It was the noise of their need to defend themselves to each other rather than hear the longings deep within themselves.

My dearest child, follow me and I will bring more healing to souls than you ever imagined possible.

Mother Again Speaks of the Taliban

January 18, 2013

Mother, do you wish me to write?

Yes, child, I am pleased that you are here to take down my dictation. Please write about the Taliban again today. There are many innocents involved in this horrible cause. Please pray especially for them today as they continue to raise children with hate and children are learning to use hate as a cause. It is of such a sorrowful hurt that I write. The Father wishes to end this kind of hate, so pray especially for them and ask the Father to bring hope to this misunderstood sect. I know this is a subject so far from you, yet so close. Innocents are being asked to do such evil. They above all other sects are most likely to say no in the second chance because of the raising of the hate to a spiritual level.

Yes, there are other so called religions and sects who teach anger at certain kinds of people, but the Taliban hate to such a degree that they feel so sure they have justification to kill and be killed. Just imagine, for example, all the martyrs who died for Christ and their assuredness that they would be with the Father. Their love for the Father earned them a special place with Him. So the Taliban believe the same, only they worship an evil god and are closed of heart. So closed of heart are they that they allow their own children to die in the name of their so called god. Please pray for them, Janine, because it was just a slight difference between them and the santeria because they worshiped an evil god as well. The only difference was the prayers of their ancestors. There are children who need prayers just as all of God's children. Some will say to hell with them because they are so evil but the Father says pray for them because of the evil that they have absorbed. Please, child, write as I dictate so that the world may understand and join you in prayer.

Now, my beautiful child, I would like to address your fears again. Please come to me as often as you like; I am here and I will always respond to you. I know there are times when you are away from here that you question my writings and love because of "noise." Please be assured that it is noise that makes you worry. Just come and write and I will make it all clear. It is in this place

Mother Again Speaks of the Taliban

that I free you from the noise. I have promised you and will continue to keep the noise out of this holy place. The time we spend together here is precious for you, I know. It is a special place of honor for the Father blesses it as well. The topic of the Taliban is one that is close to his heart as is the santeria. He wishes it to be known that prayers are needed. He has blessed you with giving me the edict to be with you in this endeavor.

Thank you, Mother, you know my heart. I know it will be time soon to tell the world of your writings. You know my heart, Mother, and soon I must bring you to my children. If it were not for the pain they will suffer when they know my story, I would have told them already.

Yes, my child, I know of your fear but do not fear, I am preparing them. I love you and yours, Janine. They are my children as well and the Father will bless them and theirs as well.

Auntie's House

Mother Teaches of the Role of Self Love and the Ego

January 19, 2013

Mother, do you wish me to write today?

Yes, my child. I have helped you to find your lost rosary and I feel your gratitude. It has such meaning for you and I too felt your angst at the loss. Slow yourself down, child, for there is no more need to rush. I am the light and the salvation and I bring you to this place so that you may know my peace. The Father moves swiftly when necessary but you need only realize I plan your movements because you say yes to me daily. So I will never ask you to rush the way you did yesterday. When you move slower, you have time to take me in. Even your sessions with souls are beginning to move slower. No need to rush. Let me plant my seeds in them and through you. You hear me louder when you slow down.

Yes, Mother.

Now to the topic of the ego; let us begin from the beginning. The Father never meant the ego to be so fearful and over protective of the human spirit. It is the same goings-on of Adam and Eve through original sin. The ego was meant to be an auxiliary component of the Spirit. It was meant to work with the Spirit in the Garden of Eden. It was meant to bring about God's will through a loving and truly conscious choice. When Adam and Eve sinned against God, they began a painful journey in which the ego split off and began to use the same ideology that the Bible speaks of. The ego bought into the idea that it is as smart and more powerful than God. So to this day it is split off from the truth and uses its power to get you to think of God as an entity that has little power in your world. That is why all souls struggle so much with the power of God. As you love and continue to love, the ego within you loses power for it can see its inevitable forgiveness. It is loosening within you, Janine, precisely because you are in concert with it and loving it.

Your dream last night was of the ego and so this topic today is not just coincidence. The Father brought you that dream so that you may see his wonder and glory. The child in your dream is your ego, young but there. The escalator was the old way of coming up

Mother Teaches of the Role of Self Love and the Ego

into your consciousness and your climbing up to me. The stairs were carpeted, which may have seemed insurmountable because of the carriage the child was in. Yet you decided to go up the carpeted stairs and you went up with such ease. There at the top of the stairs were all your ancestors and children. So you, and my hope for others who read this, will understand the Father's need to teach of the ego because the Kingdom of God is truly within, Janine.

Souls now see evil as an outside force and, yes, it is a force but it is within and coming from the ego. When we love that part of us and do not judge it but slowly and painstakingly reassure it that it need not control out of fear, then it need not tell us that we are above reproof. It is the self examination with the help of the ego that finds true peace. The ego's fear and controlling ways are loosened by the power of self love. If we continue to let a war of our two inner worlds continue, chaos continues to erupt. When we bring these two worlds together in love, we find the power of God restored to its rightful place. It is important that you understand this, child, for you will need to teach it to others.

Yes, Mother, I understand and I am aware of the love that ego and I share for you. My ego is still fearful and wants to prove to me that you are nonexistent, but I reassure her that all is well. When she tries to make me feel that you will not keep your word, I reassure her that you will bring your promises about. So like a child I reassure her that her fears are merely misgivings of the truth.

Yes, my child, I am with you and know your heart and the ego is loosening. When she told you not to trust me that the rosary was lost forever, you did not go either way. You did not tell her she was wrong and chastise her. You did not tell her she was right and it would be lost forever. You merely said let's wait and see. I have asked her to find the rosary and, if it is not found, we will find another one because it is not the rosary that is as important as the knowledge of the love of the Mother. The ego would have in the past said see, see it wasn't there (which by the way is what ego does; it comes up quickly in your mind and makes up a story), so she does not exist. Your patience loosened her and now she feels safe. Just as you set loving boundaries for a child to feel safe, the ego does as well. Loving boundaries of safety make the ego feel loved and cared for in spite of its fear.

Oh, my loving Mother, I never could have conjured up such a beautiful understanding of the ego. Thank you for making the story of Adam and Eve so clear for me to understand in this very different life we lead today.

Yes, child, different but still the same.

Mother Teaches of the Role of Self Love and the Ego

January 20, 2013

Mother, may I write for you today?

Yes, my child, I am here for you and I wish to have you write as I dictate. It is especially good to have you here tonight because it is a holiday of sorts. It is the birthday of Bernadette and it is the day the Father chose her as well. I thank the Father for her and I thank the Father for you as well. I hear your heart, my child, and I go to the Father for you and I bargain for you, so that you may be able to visit Lourdes, see her open tomb and visit the grotto where she and I met. If all falls into place, you will go but, if not, know that you will see her in the next life.

Thank you, Mother, for you truly know my heart.

Yes, my child, I know your heart. It is becoming more and more aligned with your ego and more and more aligned with the will of the Father. I also know your trepidation about how your life will change when the world is aware of my writings. Do not worry. I will take care of you and yours. You will reach many souls and the

Father is grateful for your courage and your yes in spite of all that has happened to you. You were tortured not only physically but also spiritually, for they imbedded in you such misconceptions of the Father. However, even as a child you knew of Him deep in your heart and so you are a perfect example of God's loving ways. As soon as you opened your heart as a child and invited him to come down from the Cross and be with you, He did. Yes, child, that was the day of your anointing into his love. That was the day you became open to his love. That was the day your life became holy for the Father ordained you and Don shall meet and work together, so that you might get to this day and be my voice. The angels and archangels worked with me and the Spirit so that it might come to pass. How great is the Father for He has given you so many blessings and so much hope after all the years of your lost faith. Now go and be watchful, for you will be given the opportunity to do much work for the Father.

Thank you, Mother. Thank you for all your love and blessings that you and the Father shower on me. May I be your servant in this life as well as the next?

Yes, my child, you shall. Continue your love of the Rosary for it keeps us connected. Also, come to this sacred place to write often.

Mother Teaches of the Role of Self Love and the Ego

January 21, 2013

Mother, may I be your hands today?

Yes, my child, I wish to explain your dream of last night. The flat escalator that went up two floors is the height you have risen to in these last few days and months. At the top you had initially requested a license and you had forgotten your credit card (to purchase the license). This time as well you did not have it to bring out and the woman (It was I) told you there was no credit card needed, she would take care of it. I have given you a higher understanding of my Father's ways and I have taken away any charges incurred on the way. The old application needs to be destroyed as well. So, child, do you not see that even your dreams, which may at first seem fearful, have become more and more a way of letting you know of God's love for you. I know your heart and I am pleased with you and your loving efforts.

The house on Carnation Street

Mother Speaks of the Evil in the Media

January 21, 2013

Now to get to an important issue, I wish to write of the power of the evil in the media. There is so much that the media puts an evil slant on current history that it is like an ego that has turned grandiose. The Father's people turn to it like a form of a god and feel it always to be so true. As you have seen in these last few days, there is a lot of lying going on. The Father wishes to expose this as well. It would never be so costly an issue if souls did not put stock into what the media says. It sells not only advertisements but it also sells souls an idea of truth that does not exist. Shall we stop all guns or shall we continue to sell such weapons? Shall we continue to see our neighbors the way the media presents or will we begin to see them as brothers who need *our help. Yes, my, child it is a daunting task to love all of God's children, but only when souls do, will the earth know true peace. It is not of stopping guns or trying to enslave all the mentally ill somewhere. It is the need to turn to God and all the answers will rise just as they rise in you, my child.*

It is the Father's hope and mine that the commitment to prayer will flourish and souls will be able to see the light that you see. The Father does not say that we do not need to protect the vulnerable. Not at all. He does say to bring Him into the mix and He will bring about true peace. It is my hope and wish that all souls will understand this. There is an attempt to make it all black and white and that is not possible anymore. As you take one step with the Father, it allows another step in the right direction to be taken. When you exclude Him, one step leads to another but in a wrong direction. I say to you loud and clear, my child, if all souls began to pray today, the Father would move swiftly with each step given Him and bring about peace. That being said, I go back to the media which as an entity has an ego of its own and that is a dangerous thing. The media ignores the light of the world of the Father and exaggerates the world of sensationalism. Be wary of the words they print. Ask the Father to guide you and souls into an understanding of this. Like other cults they prey on the souls of the Father and turn their individual egos hard and grandiose as

Mother Speaks of the Evil in the Media

well. As you watch and listen to the media, watch how others around you become hard and fixated on a course of action. I say to you, child, that without the Father's invited presence the world will continue to be in chaos and the media will continue to have a hold on the world.

Thank you, Mother, for letting me be your hands and as always I love you with all my heart.

I know your heart, Janine, and I bless you for coming to this holy place.

Saint Francis
Patron Saint of the Animals

Our "Flowing Relationship" and the Flow of the Book

January 22, 2013

Mother, do you wish to address Don's questions today?

Yes, my child, but first please stop for a moment and come to the Garden.

Now, my child, let us settle what you and I have. Don asks to what degree you share your personal story with that of my words to the world. They are so intertwined that they cannot be separated. Your story is the story of so many and my wish is to intertwine it with the story of my Father and his love for his children. Can you not see, my child, that it is the same? My time on earth followed a path to the Cross just as you and all souls. That path is riddled with pain and yours is just one of the stories of the many whose heart had to close to the Father. All souls feel the pain of the path laid out by Adam and Eve. All souls need to come to the Cross as you did and watch the wood of the Cross turn into a beautiful and blossoming tree. Jesus rose from the dead and souls need to remember this.

What you and I have is a special blessing given from the Father. You are given the opportunity to write my words, not because you have a special deserving personality, but because of the Father's wishes to allow his love to be brought to life. I wish the world to know that what we have is a flowing relationship. My words flow into your hands and you cannot make it up because you are not able to conjure up the ways of the Father. However, for those who do not believe let them bring their questions and I will answer. Do not attempt to answer on your own unless the peace that knows no bounds is with you. If not certain with that peace, come to me with your hands and I will answer.

As for the question about why did I not stop the abuse from happening if I was there with you from the beginning? I shall say it again. The Father sent me to you so that I might work to save you from a closed heart and also so that I might work to save those who have asked forgiveness for their part in the santeria. I, like my Father, cannot stop abuse because of the free choice of souls. When your ancestors asked for forgiveness and entered the

Our "Flowing Relationship" and the Flow of the Book

Kingdom, they began to work with angels and archangels to free the souls not only of those who committed the abuse but also those souls whose hearts were closed as victims of the abuse. This is the same question of why does God allow bad things to happen to his good people. His love is so pure that he cannot intervene in free choice. He can, however, spring into action on prayers and fasting and the Rosary. His children turned away because of original sin and the Father is working to bring all of his children home.

As for the beginning of the book, it will be helpful for Don to write of the years of his bearing witness to your journey. Week after week, and year after year, he witnessed the pain of abuse that was allowed to be released through your body and the stories that each alter told. It need not be in great detail but enough for the world to understand what your body held. A clinical perspective will help others to understand the magnitude of all those years of working through the dissociation.

As for who should read my writings next, please ask Don to allow the couple to read it as well as Dave and or the Diocese. Don needs to preface my words and your stories with his clinical perspective and then tell of your story of the surgery and Paregoric. Going all the way back to the understanding of the alters is not necessary, but an understanding of the surgery is necessary so that all will know of the intensity of the dangers of the surgery and how it made you turn to me. The dream about the Holy Family is important for that is when you realized I was in your life. Prior to that, you had no idea of my place in your life. I am aware that you have little writing skills of your own. Fear not. I will help with that endeavor.

Our "Flowing Relationship" and the Flow of the Book

January 23, 2013

Mother, may I be your hands today?

Yes, my child, go and write the beginning of the book so that souls may know how we met. I will be with you.

Yes, Mother.

mommy, my twin, me and auntie

daddy *uncle*

The Way to the Father in Today's World

January 23, 2013

Mother, may I be your hands again today?

Yes, my child, I wish to tell souls of how especially today in today's world there is a need to see the Father as a gentle loving Father who continues to search for his lost sheep. Souls need to develop a personal relationship with the Father through Jesus and that needs to take on a dialogue between them through the Holy Spirit. As you have gone, so too the Father wants to teach his children to go. It is the same path you have taken. Through Jesus there comes about a personal understanding of the Father. Through the Holy Spirit a soul can be in constant contact with Jesus and the Father. There needs to be a slowing down of the pace of your culture so that a soul can sit and listen and hear as well as speak to the Holy Spirit. There is such a loving Spirit within each of us and again that is the Spirit of God. The Holy Spirit wants to enter a soul through an invitation and then the Spirit can begin to do its work of uniting a soul with Jesus. Just as you have discovered, the words of Jesus take on a new and personal ring when we sit and listen and allow the Spirit to help us ponder.

When you know someone personally, there is so much more that gets seen and it is the same way as the Father. You can see Him in this life but not with your eyes. You see him through your heart as you do and you see Him and myself as real and in touch with your everyday goings-on. Do you see, my child, that to be in a personal relationship with the Lord brings out a knowing kind of love that expands us into the universe and all can become as one in that knowing. Knowing is what the Father wishes for his children. So to say it again, a personal relationship with God begins by an invitation to know Him and asking the Holy Spirit to aid in that endeavor. Asking for help with listening. Then it will happen.

Your generation aches for the Truth.

The church in the beginning did not encourage this type of relationship with Jesus and yet the sacrament of Confirmation is meant to do that. So, my child, it is my wish for the world to not only find time and space to ask for the gift of the Spirit, but also to ask for the gift of listening. Listening is the second step in developing a personal relationship with the Father through the Spirit and through Jesus. The listening at first brings a small voice that attests to a soul's importance, not the importance of the ego such as grandiosity, but the small voice of the Spirit. When you first heard my voice, it was a small loving voice that you felt in your heart and my voice began with loving words such as, my child, do you hear me and do you know how much I love you? Then of course the ego comes in and says you are crazy. However, with a loving inquisitiveness the loving voice gets louder and the ego gets softer. Then with time and patience you hear the movings of the Spirit loud and clear.

Mother of the grotto

Mother Shows me her Heart

January 23, 2013

Mother, do you wish to speak of our meeting today in the company of Don?

Yes, my child. It is an important part of our journey together. I asked you to share with Don my request to have you become a receptacle for me. Give witness to the pain in my heart because of the pain I see in my Son's eyes when there is a lost soul. Tell of your experience of it.

Yes, Mother, I felt your heart open and your heart joined mine. You allowed me to see the pain you feel as the Mother of Jesus and the pain you feel when one of your children says no to Jesus and the Father. I responded to your request with my yes and you gave me a personal view of your heart. For that I am truly grateful. I am grateful that you chose me to be your receptacle.

Yes, my child, I am pleased that you said yes to my request and for that I have allowed you to see into my heart. This day you took in not only my pain but also my passion to free souls from the dangers of the hell of not being with the Father.

This day Don witnessed my words directly and he also has said yes to me and the Father today. For that I am pleased. Without hesitation he said yes to my requests to both be a witness to your experience and also to write a clinical perspective. From this day forward your loving task is to work for prayers to free lost souls. Your yes has allowed me to give you this task from my heart and the pain in my heart is now embedded in you. Just as souls who have had a terrible tragedy chose to use that to try to do good, I have this day given you that passion to work towards prayers and almsgiving to free more and more souls. Do you feel that passion, my child?

Yes, Mother, you know my heart and I have absorbed your passion. For that I am eternally grateful. Please help me to be brave in the face of naysayers and grateful for those who will believe your words through me.

Fear not, my child, for I am always with you and pray for all and even more for the naysayers. Their fear is founded in the worry of the ego. Love them well, not with judgment, and all will

Mother Shows me her Heart

be well.

Yes, my Mother.

As for the book, Janine, there are a few things that need to be addressed. Yes, your mother is still alive but the truth needs to be told and I am asking you to be brave and not go back to "touch up" the truth of what happened. Your ancestors as well as your mother need to be freed from this devastating entity called the santeria. So please do not alter my words. That being said, you may omit the names of those with questions and omit the names of others who are not involved with the santeria. Also, let Don know that letting the couple and the priest to see the book is the next step. If they choose to be a part of the journey, it will be blessed; and if they do not chose to, then I will ask you to expand to other arenas.

Yes, my Mother, I love you.

Yes, my child, and my love is upon you as well. I will always be with you and yours.

The church of my ancestors

The Story of my Illegitimacy and the Dissociative Process

January 24, 2013

Mother, do you wish me to be your hands today?

Yes, my child. How beautiful are the hands that follow the Lord. How beautiful to praise Him with our body and our love. I wish to tell of the beauty of the Father and His will for you. There was once upon a time a small child who came into the world beautiful and perfect, blessed in her openness and expressed the glory of the Father, perfect in every way that infants can be. But because of the anger and hurt of her parents she was ripe for abuse. Her parents made choices based on anger and shame because that child was considered to be a bastard (that's the word once used to denote illegitimacy). That child was you, my child, and it set a process of abuse in motion.

Before I continue, I wish to let souls know of my infinite love of the children and my hope that all souls will someday work to protect infants as well as those vulnerable adults who are like children and need protection from evil.

Because of the culture of your early years, one of the greatest sins was to give birth to a child in illegitimacy. The fact that your mother gave birth to two of you (identical and so light in color) forced them to feel the humiliation of their infidelities. It began from your mother's pregnancy because they all knew of the affairs of the santeria and the sexual 'swapping" that went on. So with your birth came hatred, fear and anger for all involved, your parents and aunt and uncle. It was the santeria and their ways of thinking that made you ripe for the abuse as well. They all fell into the thinking that you were evil for showing up the adultery. If there were no second child, all might have been hidden. But there were two of you and it was then a ritual to give an evil child over to be sacrificed to the evil one; little boys as well, my child. When all was said and done, the process of your abuse and those abusive years made them all feel justified in sacrificing you.

You were so perfect, as are all of God's children. When Jesus said, come to me as a child, he meant the childlike ways which is the sincerity to be guided, the instinct to look for the beauty in the world, the beauty of their own bodies, and the beauty of the

The Story of my Illegitimacy and the Dissociative Process

Father's heart inside of them. I say also that it is a travesty when we take that away from children. That is why your prayers and those of others are needed because a heart closes when their spirit is broken. So, my child, just as you now have the passion to pray for lost souls, please include the children as well. The real travesty is the giving up of hope which leads many to commit suicide and therefore never get to see their beauty in this life.

Now, my child, go and ponder my words.

Yes, Mother. Please bless me and thank you for being with me. May I spend the rest of my life and eternity glorifying you and the Father? Also, my Mother, how excited I am to wait for your unfolding of my life. Every day now is an unfolding and I so love you.

Yes, my child, it will all unfold according to the Father's wishes.

January 25, 2013

Mother, you know my heart. Do you wish to be my hands today?

Yes, child, I know your heart and this time is for us alone. Go and write elsewhere and let all your painful feelings and questions surface. We will decide later if it is to be in print. The only part I wish in print right now is that there is such a childlike part of you that wants me to yourself and I approve of that. Come, let me hold you and sing my song to you.

Yes, Mother.

The Story of my Illegitimacy and the Dissociative Process

January 27, 2013
My Dream Last Night

I am on a retreat with Ed and he admits to an affair many, many years ago. I don't have any feelings about it either way. We walk along a path outdoors and we sit at a table with a woman. Ed has a surprising intimate conversation with her and asks, "How is your father?" I am surprised that he knows her father and I ask him if she is the one whom he had the affair with. He looks me directly in the eye and says, "Yes." I look at the woman and say to Ed, "Well, I'm glad it is her, she is a beautiful woman." I walked away in shock and two women on the path asked if I was alright. I said "Yes, but I am in shock."

I woke and went into the arms of my husband and felt hurt at the thought of an affair. When Ed appears in my dreams, it is usually the parts of me that were abused and I thought badly of myself. I thought to myself as I always do, "Don will need to explain this dream, I don't understand this one." I asked the Blessed Virgin for peace and she said: ***Spread your wings, Janine, and fly with me. Come to the heavens and I will show you the meaning of your dream.***

The wings that we took flight on showed me the dissociative process. I flew into her arms. I gave over my body (the affair) to the winged spirit and she showed me that as a child I would fixate on the statue at the grotto and dissociate, all the while seeing her face. She also showed me the somewhat likeness of my drawing to the young Virgin of the grotto. The woman in the dream is The Blessed Virgin and the two women on the path were Jesus and the Holy Spirit asking if I was alright. She told me that I actually went into shock during the abuse and that feeling was the one I experienced at such a young age.

Mother, thanks so much for the visions of the dissociative process. Once again it tells of the "Coming Home to the Mother."

The Role of "Longings"

January 29, 2013

Mother, may I be your hands today?

Yes, my child, please write as I dictate. I wish to speak of the infidelities in the world. The infidelities of men and women who are searching for the answer to their longings within their soul and that is the knowledge of the Father at the inner cellular and feeling level. They search and search and try to find it in the arms of another man or woman. You work hard at helping couples to find each other, but you also need to help them find themselves and to look at the longing in their own hearts. A couple comes together in physical and spiritual health only after they have filled the longing within themselves. Yes, you need to use the words of a clinical nature and not of God because of the secular work you do, but there is a way to open their hearts. Bring me into it and I will show you how to reach that deep part of each couple and soul.

As you are learning, so much work gets done when you help them to stop the noise. If therapists would bring me into it, Janine, then it would be easier to help couples to find their true nature and thus to find the Father. Again I say to you, my child, there is not so much need to teach of the Father's words as a need to teach how to go to the place within each of us. Then one can feel the longing and realize that it is there and cannot be filled by a spouse. Once the longing is verbalized, as you have seen, then the real work begins. I use that couple as an example again. See how without a word from you they spoke to the truth of what actually happened within themselves. They are now working in concert with each other and it happened away from the counseling session. After each was able to sit with their longings that surfaced in the session, they went home and began to work in concert and the whole trajectory of the counseling sessions have changed. Rather than fight and defend their own personal space, they now work as a loving team. How wonderful. Please use this couple as a blueprint when you try to focus solely on the surface problem solving. Bring souls into the state of longing and then the real works starts. Please remember to invite me to participate because I always need an invitation and do not interfere with your

The Role of "Longings"

choice.

Yes, Mother, I get it. I need to be aware that you need to be invited and you will show me the way to help them reach deep into their longings.

Yes, my child, it is in the longing that the Spirit rises and introduces Herself. Then with all the speed of that bullet the Spirit can work to bring that soul in concert with an open heart. Your clinical world calls it a state of vulnerability. I call it the open arms of the Spirit that is invited through an open heart. For some it will not work as quickly as the couple but do not stop praying, prayers are the fodder for the Spirit to work to open their hearts to the truth. The truth comes out in vulnerability.

I love you, Mother. May I be your hands into eternity?

Yes, my child, I will continue to bargain for you to my Father.

Janine at two at auntie's

The Terror of not Having Enough

February 1, 2013

Mother, do you wish me to be your hands today?

Yes, my child, I do. Thank you for being here and I am pleased that you are here even though you have fears and doubt that I will leave you to write on your own. My dear sweet child, have I left you yet?

No, my Mother, but I fear my own shadow some days. I need your courage to continue because I am so fearful.

Just write as I dictate, my child, and all will be clear. I have told you before that I am with you always but I know your humanness and it is the noise again. Please let me tell of the fears of all humans: There is no life after this and that it is a made up story from long, long ago. There are those who say the story of

Jesus is just a story that allows souls to have a hope of a resurrection. I tell you, my child, in a loud and clear voice that I was a virgin who gave my body and soul over to the Holy Spirit in order to do God's will. There is a Holy Land in heaven and it is filled with souls who also felt fear in the worry that there is no afterlife.

Let me tell you a story of my Son. My Son was born into a poor family and he felt the same feelings as those of poor descent today. He felt that humans have a need to look at outside possessions for comfort and a god of sorts. Even though we may tell ourselves that money has little meaning, in the very deepest part of ourselves we see it as a substitute for the love of the Father. That deep innate heart of the Father in each of us yearns to be filled with love, but we look in so many wrong places. In this way possessions are just like any other addiction, only we forget that it is a small and trivial replacement for the love of the Father.

Jesus taught his whole adult life and He never worried about the need for possessions because he trusted in the Father. Likewise we need to trust in the Father. No, it does not mean that we don't follow a path of learning and finding a means of obtaining money, but it does mean that we look inward to find the passion that the Father has imbedded in us. When a child is taught to look inside, the passion begins to rise and slowly but assuredly the passion

The Terror of not Having Enough

takes hold and the Spirit brings it about. Parents and caretakers use their own biases and try to guide a child into a possible profession that the child has no passion for, or the child has not been taught to look within. So the child chooses a path to either please his or her parents or even worse begin to define himself by going in a negative direction. I say to you, my child, please let parents of young children know that sitting with your child and looking with an open heart to what they see in their own children, rather than put their own value systems on them, is what the Father wishes. It is then that a parent can guide a child. To help a child look within is a greater gift than all the money in the world.

When there is a passion for one's work, there is an opening to the Father and an opening of one's heart. Yes, you were able today to begin to explain that albeit in a secular way, but look at the opportunities that you just opened for these patients who are looking to guide their children. There is such a fear of parents that their children will suffer if there is not enough money. So they guide their children into thinking that money is the only thing that will fill them. I say again loud and clear that you need to help your children look inside and then their passion will arise. Then the financial part will take care of itself. If all souls trusted the Father and looked inward, there would not be this terror that there will be not enough.

It is the Father who brought a child into a parent's arms and it is the Father who will guide that child to the right place. Parents need only guide their children to look inward rather than try to control their child by forcing their own fears on them. I hope to make this clear to all my children, Janine, and do not fear because your passion to do my will pleases the Father. Your passion to do the Father's will is an example of how a soul's path takes shape. As you are now aware, money has little worry for you anymore. All happens in the presence of the Father. We need only to turn to Him and that includes our children. I wish to let parents know that it is a blessing and a gift to the Father when they ask for help with their children.

The Way of Miracles

February 2, 2013

Good morning, my Mother. May I be your hands today?

Yes, my child, come to this holy place and be not only my hands this day but also my voice and heart. I come to this holy place with you to bestow my love and blessings on you and to talk about miracles. I have asked you to help me with the topic of miracles and to put miracles in the title of this book. Let me explain miracles for you and all souls. Miracles are the Father's blessings in a way that you call supernatural. They are not all seen in an instant. Some are produced over time such as the miracle of your tummy. Janine, you were given so much paregoric that it thinned the walls of your stomach and has given you digestive issues all your life. It is also what took your father for it thinned his stomach to such a point that he developed an aneurysm in his stomach. The miracle for you is that the Father has given you a healing as long as you eat the way I have taught you for now. It will all be healed soon and you will be able to profess that miracle.

There will be naysayers of course but this is a topic of miracles. There are many miracles for you, my child. You have your heart open and they will be seen. You pray for the ability to smell the roses and when your tummy is fully healed you will smell them. The wholeness of your spirit and the alters have already been realized, another miracle. Also, miracles come in so, so many other ways that it will be the topic of many conversations. Then there is the miracle of the removal of your hemorrhoid. What other miracles have happened you ask. For one your father is able to sit with Jesus not only because of his "yes" but also your prayers. This is also a gift from the Father. Miracles come in small packages or large packages. Look and listen to me, child. Do you not see my face in your heart and do you not see my hands on your hands? This is a miracle of large proportions. This is the grandest of them all, isn't it, my child?

Yes, Mother, you know how much I love being your hands. You know my heart and how I do not know the next word but trust in your promise to be the words and the hands.

Yes, my child, it is a mystery to you and I know that. It is a miracle sent from the Father and the world will know of me through you. I will be with you so do not chide the naysayers. Love them and I will be your voice when the time comes. How beautiful are your children, my child. The fact that you were given life, saved from physical and spiritual death and your "yes" has given rise to your children and grandchildren. Without intervention your ancestry would never be; another miracle, yes.

When you awoke from your surgery, did you not see my love and the Father's hands on your surgery? Had it not been for your surgery, you would not have found me in the way that you did. Your pacing and prayers brought into light your abuse and I was able to move swiftly to be with you. It was all in God's plan and all the souls needed to do this were put into place.

There are souls who also work with open hearts and say yes to the Father, so that all his plans may fall into place. That is truly supernatural, my child, and if and when all souls watch for their path to unfold rather than try to continue to look for the big bang miracle, all would be well.

Let me explain further. The Father uses miracles to bring his people to a place of openness and open heart. That being said, He brings his angels and archangels to move into the paths He has planned and to intercede for the sake of his children. He does so on the wings of prayers, the Rosary and fasting. So in this way it is a circular motion and promise from the Father. He brings about miracles when his children turn to Him in prayer and the more prayers the more miracles. You and all souls search for the big miracle to prove God's presence, but I tell you through prayer, the big miracles will give way to the even bigger miracles of love and everlasting life. However, people who do not open their hearts to the truth will continue to wait for the small ones.

There will be souls who say your hands are not a miracle right now and look for the big ones to be manifested in a researchable way. Yes, child, that will happen but it will never be enough for the naysayers. Even you, my child, wait for the "big" miracle and you have already received it. Pay attention to your hands right now. Do they not dance in the presence of my words? Could you go from word to word without an understanding in any other situation? I tell you, you could not do this without total trust in me and for that The Father and I are grateful.

So, I ask you and all souls to pray and watch with an open heart and you will witness more miracles than you ever thought possible. Remember the phone call that came from Don in an instant after you both felt there would be no extra time. That is also the way of miracles. And as you came to the keyboard today, you had no awareness of miracles as the topic I would choose for today. This is an important topic. As the miracles come, I will make it clearer for you so that souls will have knowledge of the way to search for the Father's blessings through miracles. Blessed are those who read this and are open to the world of miracles.

February 4, 2013

Mother, please hear my heart song because it is very sad right now.

Yes, my child, your sadness is of the old, old hardened ego that was responsible for keeping you safe from that unknown. I am here and together we shall love her and bring her to a place of healing. Have I not told you to come here for ego has no place here and have I not promised you my unending love?

Yes, Mother, but my ego is so fearful and she rises up like the wind and wants me to stop believing in you.

Yes, my child, I know your heart and it is a difficult journey at times. For you and those that are willing to learn the language of true love, it is a journey into bringing you home to the Father here on this earth. All my love is poured out onto you as well as all my children but you cannot find me in the everyday chaos. You will find me in the quiet recesses of your heart. You cannot find me in the misunderstandings of the ego. You come to me and the Father's Holy Spirit through Jesus and his total love for us. Your inner rumblings of the ego have given up the fight in my company as you are now aware. For those who wish to follow me, this book is a course in how to do that. It is a course in total love of every part of a soul, total love of the spirit within us, total love of the physical body you have been given, and total love of those negative parts which includes the ego. The Father has sent his blessings on you in order that this book becomes the primer for those who wish to follow me in the everyday. I am the light that comes to a soul in whatever form the Father wishes it to take.

The Holy Spirit guides each individual to its rightful place with the Father. Colors, genders, sexual preferences, or religious backgrounds have no place in the Father's plan for each of his children. All will see the Father as long as the heart opens up. The truth is Jesus died for all, no matter what origin they come from. All will be explained to the open hearted at the second chance. It is the ego that wants separation, not the Father. The ego loves the idea of separation because separation endows it with so-called higher powers. It is so grandiose that it wants you to believe I do not exist. That is what you felt today, my dear sweet Janine.

Please let my children know of my love for the whole person and that includes the ego in each of my children. For example, when you take the ego out of the equation, there is a part of a soul that will be missing. It is that part that the Father wants reunited with Him. Because it is that part that has been disobedient since Adam and Eve. But the Father wants us all to be whole here on this earth. So now it is time to love the ego and guide it back to the Father. This can only be done through love. As you can see, my child, your love for me in this place has allowed the ego to begin to loosen its grip. Is it a difficult task, yes. I say to you it is an impossible task without the Father. So when you teach, and you will, my child, teach of total love of the ego.

It is the ego that is the closest to the Father because it is the ego that has become his lost sheep. In that way the Bible comes alive in a way never expected. The words of Jesus in the Bible reflect an inner journey as well as an outer journey. Let all know that through Janine the Bible will come alive and be given a new meaning.

Jesus said, "love your neighbor as yourself" and I add to that "love yourself (your ego) as you love your neighbor (the rest of your self, the body and spirit). So now, child, I have given you and the world a glimpse into what your role is going to be. These are the miracles I speak of, the miracle of a young woman (age has nothing to do with this) who is going to be the Blessed Virgin's hands to not dispute the Bible but to make it come alive.

Mother, I have never read the Bible, all I know is what I have heard in church.

Do not fret, my child, I will teach you.

Mother of all ages, I love you with all my heart. I wish I were deserving of all your grace.

Yes, my child, I know of your heart and soul. Know that I have been given the edict to do this work with you from the Father through my son Jesus. Also, my child, notice how peaceful the ego within you is right now. When your heart is aching and fearful, bring her here and I will bring peace.

Yes, Mother.

Our Lady of Fatima

The Father's Love Despite our Choices

February 5, 2013

Mother, please let me be your hands.

Yes, child, I am pleased with your trust today. I know you are tired, my child, but you come to this place to be with me. Blessed are you for your love.

Yes, I shall talk of Bernadette for she is in your thoughts today. You ask how hard was it for her to bear witness to me and the truth. Was her love for me as intense? Yes, child, it was because she yearned to be with me as you do. She was a child and she dedicated herself to me. The world was looking for the miracle to prove that I appeared to her. Even today so many miracles occur daily and yet souls have a hard time believing in me. Her body does not deteriorate and still souls do not believe. So you ask, my child, how do I reach souls. I reach them through questioning and turning to me. I reach them by looking inward and seeing the miracle of the heart for the heart sees so much more than the eye. You need only look through your heart to see the majesty of the Father's love. I reach souls through the power of prayer.

Janine, my sweet child, your heart is burdened with wanting souls to see what you see and to find joy in this life: the joy of seeing a soul and not just a body, seeing the ego at work in a soul and loving as the Father loves, seeing his children go down a destructive path and all the while still loving them, seeing souls choose destructive paths and all the while still loving them. Letting them choose and still loving them. This is what the Father does and it is your task as well as those who wish to follow me. This is the true understanding of the Father. He so loves with an all giving love that He could not take choice away; so even when a child of the Father chooses a destructive path, his love never waivers. This is the most beautiful gift of all, Janine, and that is to love souls regardless of their choices.

And now, my child, I bring it back to you. I love you despite and because of your choices. I hope this is clear. It will take time for you are in your infancy with the understanding of the Father's ways. You are not alone, my child, and it is my wish to bring it into focus for not only you but all souls. Just as the Father so longs to

The Father's Love Despite our Choices

have his children with Him but cannot take choice away, we as souls have to accept that there are some souls who will go down a dangerous path. That it is their choice to do so. Sin does play a role as it masks true choice at times, but with prayer the Father can enlighten a soul to true choice. So, my child, your task and those who wish to follow me is one of prayer for those souls.

Your story is an example of how a closed heart opens up. You had no choice but to close your heart due to the sins of others. Through the prayer of your ancestors the Father was able to work to open your heart and you chose to turn to me. When you chose me (even as a young child you chose me), the powers of heaven were let loose. I know it is still confusing for you because there are miracles where the Father stops that kind of abuse. However, He could not stop this one until there was enough power from prayer. The santeria was such a closed evil organization that only great amounts of prayer could allow the winged spirits to move. So, does He eventually take away choice? No, never! He cannot. But He can work with prayer to move things so that the truth will be known. His love wishes only the truth to be known and your "yes" is a movement to stop not only the santeria but all such evil organizations.

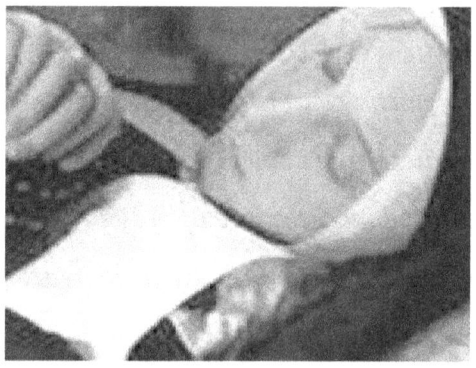

The Incorruptible Body of Saint Bernadette

Mother Speaks of Worldly Chaos

February 9, 2013

Good morning, my Mother, may I be your hands today?

Yes, my child, write as I dictate. Your heavenly Father wishes to bestow a blessing on you for you have been an inspiration to those who will wish to follow Him. He wishes to bestow a beautiful child upon you. The beautiful child within you now has blossomed to a new and holy position. Yes, my child, you feel upset because it sounds so grandiose. However, the Father wishes to let the world know that even what souls call lowly can move to a holy position in the Father's plan. You do not need to fear. Notice even now your hands glory in my words and you bless me with your heart. You work to find quiet space for us. The blessings of your fingers are a beautiful gift of the Father and each time you come to the keyboard I am with you in a very special way. This world is in chaos and yet, when you come here, it becomes clear. It is the Father's wish that all his children find such clarity. When you go back into the chaos, you bring me with you and slowly but assuredly you will be more complete. By complete I mean you will make sense even in the chaos. Let me explain. Once in the chaos it is easy to get lost in it and it begins to make sense in a superfluous way. So you need to come to me to render the chaos null.

Let me explain further, my child. There is a sect out in the world that discusses the power of positive thinking. It is not that positive thinking is bad; it is that it takes the Father out of the mix and again allows the ego to once again feel grandiose. That leaves the Father out. You like others were searching for answers about God and the universe, so you bought into it. The book "The Secret" is one such endeavor. It has sold millions precisely because of souls searching for the truth and it is dangerous because it leaves out God. That is why you and other souls need to find their own individual path to the Father in order to make sense of their own chaos. That path is what I am teaching you, my child, and that is the inward journey to the Father. Souls so want answers and they have their own answers within that the Father is so waiting to open up. Just as you are learning, my child, the chaos becomes clarity when you come here and soon you will not fall prey to the chaos. It will be important to remember that souls are in a deep search, as you are, and need to look inward to the Father for the truth. It is also important to remember that some souls are so egotistical that they are not ready to look within. That is when the power of prayer is needed.

Rather than trying to make sense to a person who is in the throes of the ego (you know this when a soul is in an argumentative state and the door is closed to listening), you pray and love because as you will see the ego loosens in the company of love. Watch as souls lock into verbal combat over any topic and see the ego at work. Then I will help you to make a loving statement. Watch what happens. I will teach you to stay away from getting caught up in the topic because ego loves that. Ego builds and builds and puffs itself up when it can force a situation that "makes itself right." Ego is so good at trying to get others to see itself as right because it is looking for acceptance and love. Remember ego is the "outsider" in a soul and is constantly looking for recognition. Even souls who do not engage openly in trying to get others to acknowledge them, do so covertly. And so, my child, it comes back to love. It is love that loosens the ego's grip on a soul and allows the Father to bring that soul home to his rightful place.

The Immaculate Heart of Mary

The True Coming Home to the Father

February 10, 2013

Mother, I brought my question to the non print page. Do you wish me to bring it here to the printed page?

No, my child, it is not necessary. The only thing I want known is that all your questions will now be answered in this way whether it be printed or not. It will be better to bring it here but I understand your fear and it will be less and less. Tell the world how I answered your question.

Yes, my Mother. Just before I came to the holy place I heard, "no, no" and felt fear. Yet when I began to ask you here with the keyboard, it all became very clear and I heard you say yes and yes to both questions.

Yes, my child, the no was the ego who was fearful. So coming to this holy and safe place and allowing me to use your fingers to answer the questions brought clarity and peace.

Now, my child, let us move to an important topic. It is one of total love and commitment of the Father to bring his children back home to Him and his loving heart, for each soul has a part of the Father's heart. When the Father sent his Son and hence a part of Himself into the world, He sent his only Son to the Cross so that all may be free from eternal damnation. Do you know what that means, my child?

I am assuming, my Mother, that it means without Jesus we would not get to know eternal life.

My, child, let me explain. Without the love of the Father, sin would not have been conquered and the war between the ego and the soul could not have been won. The Father's gift of Jesus has been the supreme act of love and only love of that magnitude can conquer sin. I am aware that souls think, "why would a loving God give his only Son up for sacrifice?" I say, my child, it is precisely because, as I have said, only love of this magnitude could save his children from choosing sin over Him. Sin (ego) gets stronger and stronger when it feels righteous and only the power of a loving Father can redeem us. My child, it is hard for you and souls to see the magnitude of my Father's love and it will be clear when you and souls meet the Father. Even "Judgment Day" is one of love for He has to dethrone the ego to bring his children home.

So please again pray and ask others to pray for this loosening of the ego. When that happens, there will be wholeness within the soul and a true coming home to the Father. The name I have chosen now has more meaning, my child, for it means a coming home of the ego to allow wholeness as well as coming home to the Father in a more pure and holy way. The Father so longs to have his lost sheep become whole with a new and loving ego that will loosen its grip on the world. Jesus said The Kingdom of God is within and I say the need to douse the flame of the ego is an inward journey as well. If all souls were able to loosen the grip of their ego the world would stop sinning and peace would reign. My, dearest sweet Janine, I say this, and I know your trepidation, but it is a story that the Father wishes to be told. His children have all that is necessary to turn evil into love and that it is within each soul.

Rules would not be needed if souls would look within and find the Holy Spirit. It is time for time is of the essence. The power of prayer can bring this about, if only souls would listen to the Holy Spirit and pray.

In the beginning, my child, there was only Adam and Eve and there was no outside force to blame for their sin. So it is to this day. It is still the inner forces within that cause evil to continue and it is only when we turn inward and stop the ego from controlling that a true returning to the Father will happen. Souls need to know, however, that it is not with more punishment and chastising that kills the evil of the ego. It is with love, love, and more love. For you, my child, your ego took on the role of anger and self loathing and only love brought you to a place of peace. The more self loathing, the more the ego had a grip and it began to loosen when love took over. Yes, this is a difficult and different way of looking at sin, but it is the truth and it is time for the truth to be revealed, my child. My Father wishes to let all souls know of his love and He loves with purity and mercy. His love is unwavering. His lost sheep need only turn inward and lean on the Holy Spirit and sin will end.

Mother, is there anything else you wish to write about today?

Yes, my child, write about love and how easy it becomes when it is in the name of the Father. For no matter how sin takes its course in a soul, the Father's love is all encompassing. When you turn to his Son through the Holy Spirit, all sins are not only forgiven but used by Jesus and the Spirit to bring about healing. Let me explain further. Turning to me or Jesus or the Spirit brings a powerful prayer that the Father uses to send his angels and archangels to bring help and peace to the soul. Then the ego will learn to love. The Father smiles upon his children who turn to Him, no matter the degree of sin. Of course those with hardened egos will find it hard to turn to Him. With the power of prayer of others, healing of the ego can take place. It is as I have said before, those souls who are healthier need to turn to the Father. Giving over of themselves to the Father not only brings salvation for themselves, but it becomes a powerful prayer for others. Your prayers and your yes has brought you as well as so many others salvation.

Thank you, Mother, for allowing me to be your fingers. I love you with all my heart. Thank you for your blessings on me. May I always serve you!

Janine Lariviere	Coming Home to the Mother

Our Lady of Lourdes

Mother's Prayer for all Souls

February 12, 2013

Mother, may I be your hands and fingers today?

Yes, my child. Let us pray together today. Holy Father, bless all souls today that they may find you in the inner recesses of their hearts and may all souls learn to value themselves as you value them. May all your children learn of your intense love for them and may all souls reach heaven. Father you gave up your only Son so that all may be freed from the bonds of sin and may they choose you at the second chance. Father most powerful Creator, send your angels and archangels to witness to the pain of souls and to aid in the safe return of your children to their rightful place in your loving plan. Amen.

Our Lady of Mount Carmel

The Misguidedness of Adam and Eve Explained

February 13, 2013

Now, my child, let us move to another topic and that is the topic of original sin which I have said before is that of disobedience to the Father. The ego chose to take its own course and became grandiose and felt it could do better without the Father. Like a child who begins to develop a want for autonomy, Adam and Eve wanted autonomy; only Adam and Eve didn't get it right. The Father had already given them autonomy in the Garden of Eden but they didn't realize it because the ego brought a false promise of "more." Like a child who stubbornly shakes off the guidings of a parent in order to gain autonomy, souls strayed from the Father in that way. But, unlike a child who accepts guidance, Adam and Eve chose to not follow the Father's guidance.

The egos of children need loving guidance and not punishment, just as the Father chooses to guide his children in the most loving of ways. That is with total love. Right from the very beginning the ego began its sinful ways and gave the soul the grandiose idea that we do not need God to help. As you witnessed yesterday (which is the way so many, many souls see God today), the young man who had such a terrible loss could not cry. He had taught himself through his ego to be so strong that he need not feel the pain of such a loss. The "I can do this by myself" as well as "I will disappoint people if I cry" is the grandiosity of the ego at work. Your witnessing to the pain allowed his ego to soften and a few tears flowed. That is the way of the Father, my child. He cannot stop the pain but He can bear witness to it and heal it. Yes, there is pain when we suffer such a loss but there is also the beauty of healing when we are in the company of the Father. Souls need to aid each other by bearing witness to the pain of another and in so doing provide the same healing as the Father. In that way, souls help the Father to bring his people inward to the deepest part of themselves and hence meet the Holy Spirit.

Let me say it again so all souls will understand this. We become an instrument of the Holy Spirit when we witness another's pain or loss and or even misguidedness. It matters only

The Misguidedness of Adam and Eve Explained

that we bear witness to the longings of another. We need not put our own "spin" on another soul's "story." We need only listen and let the Holy Spirit reach down and introduce Himself. Do you now see, my child, you need not give answers as to how to "feel better" or how to "make it better with a change of attitude?" This closes a soul rather than opens it. Souls need to listen and bear witness and not "fix" and all will be well. Rather, the Holy Spirit enters a soul who feels heard and listened to. Ponder my words and begin to bring the idea of witnessing into your practice and watch the miracles happen. This is not just the work of a therapist, my child, it is the work of all souls who wish to follow me as well as find true love and peace on this earth.

daddy and his siblings at auntie's house 1944

The Ways of a Loving Family

February 14, 2013

Mother, I come to be your hands today. Do you wish to have me write for you?

Yes, my child. I come to tell the truth of God's plan for his children and that is to have everlasting life with Him and the Holy Family. Let us talk of the love of a holy and righteous family. If a loving family wishes to follow the Father, they need to follow a path of love. The truly righteous family brings guidance to children through love and a loving family prays and has family discussions about the Holy Family. Discussions with children must take into account the Blessed Trinity so that children hear of the world of the Father on a more consistent basis, not just relegated to Sundays, if at all.

The old church teachings did not encourage reading the Bible and having discussions about it, but I say to you that the truth of the Bible comes alive when we talk about it in a way that makes it relevant today. That is precisely why I am asking you to write. I am the light of salvation and I bring a relevant truth to the world, for the Father has decreed that it is now time. You are my child and I shall bring the truth through you.

I guarantee a beautiful life on this earth, if families begin to discuss the gospels with their children. Children above all others can see the miracles for they are not bound by the hardened ego that makes it hard for adults to see the truth of the Father's world. There are so many beautiful stories in the Bible that children can understand, such as the story of God saving his people in Egypt and the parting of the waters. Janine, this is the beginning of more and more discussions on how to help families find their way in such a turbulent world.

Just as you have witnessed today, the world wants nothing more than to help you get lost in the insanity and the chaos. When you come to this holy place, take a moment to put your cares away and place your trust in me. This is the beginning of the way of my path to the light and the Father through Jesus. We shall call it "The Coming Home to the Mother" for this is the path through me to Jesus and the Father, coming home to the Mother of salvation. Yes, my child, it is not only a book that I write but a path as well. In coming home to me souls come home to the Mother's heart. The love that I bring for the world is so in need of unconditional love. No more fire and brimstone and chastising but true love that guides.

I wish to let souls know that my writing through you takes an important yes on your part. You come here with love and at times I ask you to say "we" for you are a part of this path and this book, my child. No, it is not a matter of deserving, it is a matter of grace and all you need do is thank me.

mommy and daddy in 1940

The Steps in Coming Home to the Mother

February 14, 2013, Continued

The first step in coming home to me is to take time and teach the children to stop and take the time rather than accept the idea that boredom will take over when we stop. Children can and will stop if their parents stop. So the first part of the path to coming home of a soul to its rightful place in the Father's plan is to stop and ask for guidance from me. I shall bargain with the Father for all souls. When you stop and ask for help and guidance, I will help with my loving heart and I will aid in loosening the grip of the ego so the noise will lessen and lessen. However, the first step is to stop and pray for guidance. When you stop even for a few moments especially as a family, you invite the truth of God's love into the family. This is so rarely done that children get the idea *that it is in the background and not the foreground.*

I wish souls to know that at this juncture of the journey you are still in your infancy and you are learning to trust me. So, now as souls read this they can embark on the same journey and have a guide in you. You too are beginning to trust me in new ways. Let all souls know that, when the noise arises, it does so like the wind and you get pulled into a tornado at times. But each time you turn to me with love, I show you the path back to me.

Thank you, my Mother. Thank you so much. I will spend the rest of my life working to be your hands as well as your student. You know me, Mother, and you know my heart and I am so young in all this and so child-like in so many ways. You have taken away all my ideas of how the world should work and now I am a blank slate. So do what you will with me, for I am no longer bound by the ideas of this world except for my fear of not pleasing you.

I know your heart, my child, and yes you have had to let go of all your past. Now you are ready to begin to follow me in ways you never could have known given your shaping. I am here and, as I teach you, others will be able to learn from your experience.

So souls who wish to follow me need only stop and turn to me to begin.

The Steps in Coming Home to the Mother

February 18, 2013

Mother, may I be your hands today?

Yes, my child. I wish to talk about you today so that souls will know the work you do and the hardships you bear. The dream of last night means nothing more than your fear of having to let your story be told to the world. Yes, it takes much courage and trust in me and the Father. I am aware of this and do not fear, it will all be blessed. You have such fear and I have promised you I will be with you when you share your story especially with your daughters. I wish the world to know of your pain at having to tell your daughters this story for they never had to be told of the horrors before. All they knew was that you went to therapy for abuse by your father. I am preparing them but I know of a mother's fear of hurting and traumatizing her children. For that I wish the world to know of your bravery. It is causing so much fear that you hesitate to come here. I wish all souls to know that it is especially when you have such fears that you need to take it to me or my Son.

My dear sweet child, your story mingled with my guidance will set many souls free. Blessed are those that will read this and take my guidance to heart and follow me, for my way brings peace and everlasting life. Peace on this earth as well as everlasting life in the next. Breathe in my love and peace, child. Take heart, I am with you and continue to bless and work through you. My guidance is always with love and the love of my Son brings me here with you. I had to see him hurt and die so that you may have everlasting life. So I know, my dear sweet Janine, the pain in a mother's heart when her child is traumatized. Teach them to turn to me and all will be well.

Yes, my Mother. Thank you for the peace you bring to me today and please open the doors that are necessary for me to tell my children and the world.

Trust in me, my child, it will all unfold as the Father wills. You need only to keep turning to me and saying yes.

Yes, my Mother.

Now, my child, to address the issue of tolerance; tolerance is not just tolerating others by reason of color or sexual preference. It is also tolerance of oneself in that we need to tolerate our insanities that arise. This does not mean giving way to them. It means tolerating them while the Father and I do our work. For you, my child, you need to tolerate the irrational statements of

The Steps in Coming Home to the Mother

your ego that so wants to get you to buy into the idea that you do not matter. When tolerance takes over, there is no fight. Just allow the ego to make its statement and lovingly listen to its underlying plea. For you that underlying plea is "please hear me for me there is no hope, there is no afterlife because I am so horrible that you cannot have everlasting life." For you and others like you, my child, that plea brings up the ego's grandiose idea that she has had all the control and hence wants you to believe that there is no hope.

Grandiosity comes in all forms and for you it took the form of telling you that you have no meaning. It is a hardened thought and it will take time to loosen it enough for it to join you. I say to you to listen to the justifications of your ego and stop pushing it down. She becomes stronger when you do that.

This brings me to the second step in following me, my child, and that is to listen. Listen to the ego, listen to me and listen to others. Listening without judgment brings all the noise into one bowl. When you turn to me, I can and will help you and all souls to sort things out. As you can attest, it is a very difficult task and impossible without me but with me or the Spirit it becomes a labor of love. It turns into love of self, love of me, and love of others. I am asking you to work on this and with my help it will happen. So now, my child, you have been able to turn to me in all things and the next step is to listen.

Yes, my Mother, I will listen and the hardest of all is to listen and love my ego child because she is so full of fear and despair.

Yes, my child, I am aware of your ego-child and I will call her the ego-child as well. Go and love her as I do.

Yes, my Mother.

The Steps in Coming Home to the Mother

February 19, 2013

Mother, may I be your hands today to help let the world know of your tremendous love?

Yes, my child, I am aware of how you feel my love today. I am the Mother of salvation and I bring a new and glorious truth to the world in a way never spoken of before except when my Son said "Love your enemy." I say love the enemy within and with prayer. In turning to me souls will become whole and will return to the Father in a new and glorious way. Continue to practice coming to me and listening and it will become pure joy in time. I can and will bring wholeness to those who understand my plea for prayer, sacrifice, and the Rosary. Sacrifice in your terms is nothing more than taking time to listen. In your world that becomes a difficult task and hence a sacrifice from the pull of the world. So, my child, as you begin to listen with a new ear, describe your experience.

Yes, Mother. At first all the noise was deafening, the sound of the light, the sound of the cars, the sound of my heart, the sound of silence. Then I began to experience some anxiety at the noise because it was so deafening. After that I experienced peace and a new vitality especially towards prayer. I was able to look at prayer as a new beginning. A new beginning into the world of being in your presence despite the noise and I experience you in all things even the noise. My ego-child did not fight me in this practice and that was at first confusing but now I know she is taking it in and beginning to relax some of her fears. Her voice is not so loud today.

Yes, my child, that is the way of listening. It brings you not only inside yourself but outside as well. The noise you speak of is all consuming at first, but just think of how it numbs souls to what is actually going on in the world. There is a beauty beyond the noise that takes you outside yourself so that you can listen with a new ear. That beauty is that of my Father and the Holy Spirit and the road to Jesus, my Son. I come to you in a special way but all souls can find their own inner Holy Spirit in whatever form that the Father has decreed for that soul. Practicing listening is difficult, given all the noise. But with the help of the Holy Spirit it can and will be done. This is why learning to listen is so important for it opens up both the inner and outer world to the Creator. Go and listen with your new ear and take it all in. Then come back for I have more for you and all souls.

The Steps in Coming Home to the Mother

Later in the Day

Mother, do you wish me to write?

Yes, my child, tell of what you have learned today.

Yes, Mother, I felt myself getting angry at my husband for no apparent reason other than I didn't want to hear what he had to say. I asked myself why and I heard the ego-child within me begin to make angry statements about him. I told ego-child it was alright and that I love her. I asked why was there such anger because my husband was merely telling the truth about a situation. Yet I felt a strong feeling of anger (In the past the angry feeling would take over and I would get quiet and chastise myself for feeling angry). I asked ego-child what was wrong and why was it so upsetting to hear the truth.

What I got was an insight of major proportions. Ego-child told me of all the lying that I had witnessed from my mother and how I was forced to lie to keep her from hurting me. I had to agree with her twisted thinking (it felt normal at the time) or face her wrath. I began to remember telling outright lies because she could not tolerate the truth about anything. I was forced to agree with her when she would say terrible things about my siblings, relatives and neighbors. My father would make us lie to keep the peace as well. So, ego-child made sense of the lying for me. It all happened because I let her have a voice rather than push her down or even worse act it out.

So, Mother, I can now attest to the fact that ego loosens in the presence of love. How great you are for showing me the way to the wholeness that you have promised.

My child, you have done well for I know how your love is growing for yourself and that pleases the Father. Your act of humility in telling this story is the beginning of a beautiful teaching experience for others, so that they may have a blueprint of the need to listen. Go and listen with your new ear.

The Steps in Coming Home to the Mother

February 21, 2013

Mother, please let me be your hands today.

My child, rest with me for a few more minutes and express your sorrow and pain. Then read the story of Job. Let your ego-child try to get you to believe that I am wrong about the hemorrhoid. Reassure her and then come back to me and you will be free again.

Mother, the story of Job is that God allowed Satan to test Job because he wanted Job to be strong, thereby proving he was not a hypocrite. Job proved himself to be true to God.

Yes, my child, that is basically it. And so now with your permission I would like to compare Job to you.

Yes, my Mother, your will be done.

You were tested today and were asked to accept my healing of your hemorrhoid with an act of faith because the doctor could not prove or disprove that fact that the large hemorrhoid was removed. There were no fissures nor was there a large hemorrhoid. You became fearful that you could not prove it, so souls would see you as a fake. It is a matter of faith and trust, my child, for it was necessary to remove it so that your digestion can return to normal, given your rare cyst and your thin walled stomach. Yes, you were tested but you did not fail me, my child. What does it matter what the world thinks as long as you stay faithful like Job did. Did the Father test you like Job? No, not at all, but like Job you have remained faithful even in the light of those who may criticize you. Despite the rantings of your ego-child you have stayed faithful to me. Your ego-child wants to do what Job's ego-child did: to prove Job was a fake, that in the long run he was too superficial to stay true to God. This is a test of all souls, Janine.

All souls have that ego-child that wants to test a soul's faithfulness. Just as Satan was not able to pressure Job, so you too and souls who follow me will need to trust with a child-like faith and to reassure ego that all is well, that you are the rock of my Father's love. No one can make you stray from the truth of the Father's love. The truth for you is that there was a healing that night. Your body burned for over four hours and your digestive issues are almost totally healed because of it. Have faith for it will all heal in the Father's "time." Notice how interchangeable the names Satan and ego-child are, my child. It is all the same but it makes it more understandable in your time to see the working of sin through the ego. It is the ego within that is the cause of sin. So sin, Satan and ego are all interchangeable.

I also wish the world to know, my child, what you have been through today and that is a turning to me and the love you have displayed for your ego-child. Yes, it was tormenting but you turned to me and like Job the Father is blessing you for your faithfulness.

February 22, 2013

Mother, thank you for the grace today. The grace to do your will is to bear witness to so much pain. There is so much pain in some of the souls I work with, the pain of losing a loved one as well as the loss of a relationship. Thank you for your blessings and strength. I can't do it without you. Mother, can you address why I feel so lost and confused.

Yes, my child. You are lost because of the blank slate that you spoke about. You are more vulnerable because of it as well. That is why it is important to come here often for I will be with you and teach you my ways. Your ability to listen with a new ear is precisely because you have let go of the old ways of thinking. The anxious feelings are because everything is so new and yet is clearer than ever before. Your ego-child, however, is having the hard time for she is also so confused by love that she is recoiling and fearful. We must go slowly until ego-child loosens again. Love her with all your heart right now so she loosens. Do not

The Steps in Coming Home to the Mother

chastise. Listen with your new ear. She is so sure that you will be labeled a fake and her "reputation" as the perfect one will be damaged. The role of ego is to deny truths in order to preserve the idea that somehow the ego-child is perfect. But only the Father is perfect. This again brings us to the fact that ego was the sinful force in the story of Adam and Eve. Ego is like the prodigal son when he or she returns to the Father. The heavens rejoice in the soul's return home of the true and holy part of ego, the part the Father initially espoused into a soul. The loosening of your ego-child is happening, my child, but it is a long journey for ego to come home. So you need to be patient. As I have said before, ego needs reassurance that my truth is the better way.

Now, my child, I would like to discuss the topic of ego on a more intimate issue. Ego is that narcissistic part of all souls. It feels it knows all the answers and is above the lessons of the Father. Please tell of our visit together today.

Yes, my Mother, I had anxiety and asked that we sit together awhile. As we did, you asked me to ask ego-child to enter my heart and enter the Garden with us. I immediately felt an unburdening of my soul. Ego-child began to yell and try to convince me that as always there is no hope. No hope of resurrection, no hope of an everlasting life and no hope that men would ever respect women without lustfulness. It was then that ego entered my heart and, instead of fearing her, you showed me the way to love her and not judge her. Ego-child has stopped the ranting and has "felt" the love in my heart perhaps for the first time. I so pray that all souls can feel this love even for a moment because it feels just like the rapture. I float in peace and in your loving company. Mother, only you can bring this kind of peace and it only comes in your loving company. Mother, My Mother, please help me to bring ego-child into my heart more and more. Help me to continue to listen to her narcissistic wounds. I never realized before what a negative feeling that word used to bring. I've always felt it was such an awful sin to have narcissistic tendencies but now I know it is the wounded ego-child who somehow wants to return home but cannot find a path. Now I realize I am the path. With your loving help it will happen.

Yes, my dear child. Your peace is a special blessing for the peace you feel has no boundaries. Yes, it is rapture. Your loving heart has been able to allow ego-child to feel safe enough to enter your heart rather than cause such an anxious uproar within you. Child, I wish the world to know that this is part of the process of turning to me. Ego has a way of getting louder and louder and protests more and more as you turn to me and become my child. It is temporary as the sinful ego lets its wounds be confessed in a loving environment. Then it will heal. You have followed my path and, yes, it is frightening. The ego has generations of sinfulness

The Steps in Coming Home to the Mother

attached to it, but it is important to keep returning to me and I will help the Father's love be expressed in my loving presence.

My dear sweet Janine, have you not noticed the letting go of your restrictive boundaries as well? You are able to see the beauty of allowing me to be your boundary and that is that there is no boundary to my love. My heart is so open and it has no boundaries. That is what you are feeling. I wish that for all my children. Their stories are different but my promise is the same: that is an open heart which has no boundaries, for my spirit has no boundaries. There is no other work for the rapture except that your heart is so open it reflects my heart as well. I bring peace and not angst. I bring hope and not hopelessness. I bring rapture and not condemnation. The condemnation comes from your ego and I have been able to show her your love today. You are right. She responds to your love and all souls need to understand this. The rapture can be a gift to all who follow me for I am the light of salvation. I open all hearts through souls who follow me. In so doing the ego's wounds heal and loosen.

February 26, 2013

Mother, I wish to thank you for being with me this weekend and your loving connection to me and my children. My heart has been opened to ego-child. She has nested in my heart and has loosed her grip of fear. Underneath the "know it all attitude" she is riddled with fear and, when I invite her into my heart, those fears lessen. My heart is still so open and so in love with you and your teachings. Your love and guidance are truly amazing. Words cannot describe the openness of my heart to you and all your guidance. I will spend the rest of my life praising you.

Yes, my child, I know your heart and that of the ego-child who is returning home to the Father. The original role of ego was to nestle into the heart of each soul and to be a voice inside the heart. Ego was meant to bear witness to the Father through the Father's loving heart. The ego that sinned against the Father lost itself in the mind and never looked back. It does not know of love until it arrives in the heart. Then it loosens and begins to feel the

The Steps in Coming Home to the Mother

total love of the Father for love comes through the heart. The heart has a voice and ears.

When it opens the way you and I have worked to open it, there is a knowing and a peace that knows no bounds. That is the feeling of your open heart right now for it has no bounds. This is the task now to remain open and in connection with your ego through the heart. Ego now has its place and that is to be with you in the internal world of the Father. Together you make up the total heart of the Father. The ego can now be a part of you in a beautiful and loving way without battle. A true wholeness can now be achieved and a true coming home to the Mother and Father can happen.

The coming home of yourself and your ego into your heart is also a mastering of the feminine and masculine. A union of both is the Father's design, my child. Souls who find the wholeness I speak of may discover this union in a slightly different way. The union is the same; a union of the masculine and feminine. Your ego-child will be the one to lead you into a more perfect union with the Father. She contains the masculine in you. Without her, true wholeness cannot occur. Yes, my child, it is time for you and all souls to see and understand the Father's role of the ego which is to provide a deep understanding of the need for wholeness within the heart. It is the inner journey to a union not unlike the union of man and woman in the outside world. This inward journey through the heart between the self and the ego provides the same kind of intense love that a sexual union provides. Only this one will bring joy that knows no bounds. It is a love that passes through the heart and opens itself up to the entire world. The Father meant it to be a lasting and loving inner relationship between the masculine and feminine, so that in a deep knowing way each soul would have the blueprint to know their beloved other. Sadly, the ego ran away with itself but the Father so wishes each soul to find that blueprint again. For you, my child, you and ego-child are both home together in a way you could never imagine. That is why I did not answer your question about men, for you now will discover it in a deep and meaningful way through your ego-child. You will learn by listening with your new ear and using your new voice with ego-child.

Yes, my child, let me say it again for you. The ego is the other side of your deep inner self. It was designed by the Father to make a loving wholeness within the heart so that all souls on a very deep and innate level would know both the masculine and feminine. It was meant to provide a level of knowingness of the Father's heart. You will now get all your answers as to what drives men, just as men who follow me will be guided to understand women in a deep and innate way. Just let me

The Steps in Coming Home to the Mother

acknowledge that this applies to the homosexual community as well, for there is a need to incorporate both the masculine and feminine as well. I will guide you more on that later. For now, my child, revel in your new-found understanding of ego.

February 28, 2013

Mother, may I be your hands today?

Yes, my child, come to me for I am the light that shines through your heart and I will lighten your journey to the Father. Come and be my hands, arms and heart to all who pass through your life, for all that pass through you will be given blessings as well. You and souls so wish for the miracles and with your help souls will see them in a unique and loving way.

The Father brings his children to a special loving place when they follow Him without reservation and are willing to be guided by the light. The light comes in many forms, my child. It comes in the form of consciousness and awareness of the truth that is embedded deep within us. It comes in the form of knowledge of the Scriptures. It comes in the form of listening to the wounds of others. It comes in the form of prayers for others or ourselves. It comes in the form of turning to me or my Son and asking for the

The Steps in Coming Home to the Mother

way to the Father. But most of all, it comes in the acceptance of the duality that the Father has embedded in each soul. That is the ultimate light. When the two come together as one, it not only reunites the masculine and feminine but it brings into the light the true meaning of the Father's wish for each soul. When the masculine and feminine within each soul comes together, it is the redemption that Jesus speaks of. Sin no longer has hold for the ego has come home and it is in union again with the loving Father.

Redemption, my child, is meant to be had here on earth and not only in the next. Look at how free your heart is and how easily ego slides into your heart. Your dream last night was the slipping away of the hardened ego-child and she went missing because she is gone. The only thing you need do now is to be sure to come to your holy place daily, for the pull of the earth may give ego the idea again that it has no worth. I promise you and all souls who come to me daily with a turning to me will not lose the light of salvation in this world or the next, for the heart will be so open it will always say yes to the Father.

The miracle of the unfolding of your life is a gift to others who will need help and courage to turn to me. As you now are aware, my dearest Janine, the turning to me and listening are the necessary ingredients to following me and the Spirit of the Father and the Son. For you, my child, this book has been a journey from the depths of a living hell to the joy of my love. Know that each soul has its own unique journey and so each soul has its own way to me or to my Son or to the Holy Spirit. You reach the Father in any of these ways. For you, my child, you needed my loving arms in order for you to be able to see and love your ego. She was so hardened to the masculine side because of the abuse that only I could have brought you into a total union with the ego-child. She is now a part of you and she will blossom as you and she begin to see the world through the Father's design.

And so, my child, this is the end of this part of the book, but I will continue to use you and your hands to aid souls in finding me. For now work with Don to get my words published. This is the primer for souls who wish to follow me.

For now end this portion and we will begin anew tomorrow. It is my wish to have you test the waters of the outside world.

Yes, my Mother, be it done unto me according to your word.

The Miracle of the Feather

December 6, 2013

My mother passed on Thursday, December 5th, 2013. On the day of her death as she lay unresponsive, I began to tell mom of the Blessed Virgin's promise to me that she will be with mom when she passes over and there will be dancing in the Garden. All she need do is say "yes" to the Mother of God. I kept telling mom over and over again of Mother Mary's promise that she will bring her into the presence of her Son, Jesus. I whispered in her ear that we needed to have a secret just between the two of us. I asked if she would let me know when she is in heaven and safe with her ancestors. I asked mom to please send me a feather when she was in heaven. In the last few hours of her life, my twin sister joined me and we sat on mom's bed, one on each side of her. We sang and prayed together as mom slipped away. I leaned in to mom and asked if it was, "OK to tell our secret?" I then told my sister about the feather and we both asked mom to send us a feather. Then mom passed and as she did she opened her eyes and we were able to say goodbye before she took her last breath. We told her we loved her and we read her lips as she said she loved us too. She then passed peacefully.

Early on Friday morning, the feather you see below was found on the passenger side of my sister's car. Our mom is in heaven and she is OK and we can't keep the secret. It belongs to all who believe in miracles. Yet another miracle from the Blessed Virgin. Thank you so much, Mother, for bringing our mom home to you and the light of your womb.